OFF
COURSE

OFF COURSE

FIVE LESSONS FROM THE LIFE
OF A NONCONFORMIST

BY CONNOR BERNAL

NEW DEGREE PRESS
COPYRIGHT © 2021 CONNOR BERNAL
All rights reserved.

OFF COURSE
Five Lessons from the Life of a Nonconformist

ISBN   978-1-63676-528-0 *Paperback*
        978-1-63676-067-4 *Kindle Ebook*
        978-1-63676-068-1 *Ebook*

This book is dedicated to my family, who always encouraged me to find my path in life. To all of you, I love you.

CONTENTS

AUTHOR'S NOTE		11
CHAPTER 1.	THE LECTURE SERIES	17
CHAPTER 2.	KUWA HURU	27
CHAPTER 3.	GODDESS OF THE SKY	55
CHAPTER 4.	ISLES OF THE SEA	87
CHAPTER 5.	WAVES	117
CHAPTER 6.	THE SCHOOL	139
CHAPTER 7.	THE LAST LECTURE	163
ACKNOWLEDGMENTS		171
APPENDIX		173

"To be yourself in a world that is constantly trying to make you something else is the greatest accomplishment."

—RALPH WALDO EMERSON

AUTHOR'S NOTE

In 1968, Yvon Chouinard set off with his friends on a road trip that spanned from California to the southern tip of South America. On their adventure, Chouinard experienced some of the coolest life events you and I could ever dream of, like surfing down the west coast of South America, summiting mountains in the Andes, and unforgettable exchanges with locals. This journey resulted in incredible life lessons that one could only obtain in this way.

Chouinard did this in his late twenties when the world was probably telling him to get a real job, pursue higher education, or do whatever someone his age should be doing. Nevertheless, he ignored these pressures. Despite the opportunity cost of his voyage and the possibility of returning to a life with no clear direction in the professional world, Chouinard chose to follow his own path and trust that it would all work out for him in the end.

Well, it did. You might not be familiar with his trip or recognize his name. However, you will recognize the name of the company inspired by this adventure, which turned him into a billionaire businessman—Patagonia.

Chouinard's story is a good example of what we, the young generation, are currently facing—pressure to conform. Instead of pursuing our passions, we feel pressure to conform to society's expectations and move on with life before taking the time to enjoy it. We push ourselves through years of school with no break, we begin careers we don't really like but feel like we need, and we join friend circles we don't actually enjoy. We eventually find ourselves in some form of an identity crisis, questioning who we are and where we are going in life.

This identity crisis is evident when we look at the mental health trends of our age groups. One study showed that the physical and mental health of millennials in the US is declining so rapidly that mortality rates could rise up to 40 percent higher than those of Gen X without intervention.[1] Millennials have also been tagged as *job-hoppers*, with over 20 percent reported having changed jobs within the last year and six of ten currently open to new opportunities, says Gallup. They are also the least engaged at work.[2]

The subsequent generation, Gen Z, also faces similar issues. One study found that 55 percent of Gen Z subjects reported their mental health was below very good or excellent, the

---

[1] "The Health of America," Blue Cross Blue Shield, published November 6, 2019.
[2] "Gen Z More Likely to Report Health Concerns," American Psychology Association, accessed August 21, 2020.

lowest score of all age cohorts.³ Though little data exists to show their performance in the workplace, one can only imagine these negative trends will continue.

Of course, a myriad of reasons could explain why the young generation faces declining mental health outside of conformity pressures. However, it's hard to deny that even amidst new waves and embraces of individuality, the young generation is crumbling under pressure to fit a mold.

I felt these pressures as a college student at my university's business school. I was constantly feeling pressure from my peers to drown myself in work, take up another internship, give up my summer to build my résumé, and work for any company with a big name just to make myself more marketable. I'd have to slave away for a few years, but the hard work now would pay off later.

But there was a problem. I had spoken with many older mentors who had been in the exact same position I was in and had listened to that same advice I was receiving. In hindsight, though, they wished they hadn't. They regretted rushing into important life decisions in those formidable years without asking themselves if it was right for them. Many wished they had been brave enough to take up a career that was more suited for them instead of a safer, more secure career.

In addition to their advice, I couldn't ignore my own deeply rooted feelings that the traditional paths were not for me. I

---

3   Amy Adkins, "Millennials: The Job-Hopping Generation," Gallup, accessed August 21, 2020.

always felt the powerful desire to embrace what made me unique, and that desire always pushed me to choose a life course that was right for me, regardless of whether it was popular or not. I looked to examples of Yvon Chouinard, Steve Jobs, and others who had also made unique life decisions that probably seemed strange at the time. Something inside these individuals had encouraged them to step outside of their bubble and follow their hearts, which led to powerful realizations about the world and life that propelled them forward to success.

I, too, decided to ignore the pressures of the world and follow passions of my own. I had always dreamed of traveling the world and interacting with other cultures from around the globe. While balancing my studies, I spent what little money I had to travel whenever possible, and I became actively engaged in service and humanitarian organizations both in my community and abroad. My travels made me aware of the vast economic disparity between my life in the US and life in other countries, which ultimately led to my finding a prestigious job with a company committed to solving those problems.

The decisions I made in those foundational years to take my own path helped me find my calling in life and set me on a course that was right for me. I ended up being able to enjoy life in my younger years to the fullest, discover what I was passionate about, and still end up with a great job. Just how things worked out for Yvon Chouinard, they've also worked out so far for me too (though it might take me a few more years to become a billionaire).

I desperately wanted to do something to help the young generation see the beauty of choosing to embrace their individuality. I wanted to help millennials realize it's not too late to live out their passions while helping Gen Z learn from the mistakes of previous generations and course correct before it was too late. Most importantly, I wanted to help them realize that by choosing not to conform, they could open up a world of new discoveries and life lessons catered to them to help in their personal journey.

It was here that my book was born. I took the lessons I had learned on my adventures around the world, all the good that came from my nonconformist approach to life, and I told them through the story of a boy named Jaime—all with the intent that you too could see the benefit of choosing not to conform so you could follow your passions and open the door to endless possibilities.

I chose to fictionalize the story instead of telling it in the first person so you wouldn't feel like my book was just a call for attention and an attempt to say, "Look at me!" It would be quite ironic to encourage my audience to live a nonconformist life by mimicking mine.

With that said, I want to emphasize that this book is not about travel. The objective of this book is to encourage people to follow their passions and see the good that comes as a result. I use travel to illustrate this idea because, for me, that was my classroom. Though the discovery of my important life lessons came on my travels around the world, your discoveries can happen anywhere. It is not about where you uncover life's hidden lessons but how you find them that matters most.

In conclusion, I invite you to discover the power of nonconformity. Make the decision to live a nonconformist life and see what follows. I promise it will be worth it.

We don't have to conform to the world's expectations to fit a mold. We don't have to surrender to a single path to *success* simply because infinite paths lead there. Choosing to conform will likely cause you to feel unfulfilled, empty, and at a loss of individual identity. Only through nonconformity and following your heart will you reach the true happiness and fulfillment you seek.

One last note that I feel is important to address is that nonconformity is not about rebellion. Anyone trying to use nonconformity to justify breaking the rules or bringing down a system has not understood this book. Nonconformity is about finding your own path, not tearing down others.

It is my hope that through Jaime's journey you will find inspiration to be a nonconformist yourself, create the path in life in which you wish to live, and find meaning that will give your life purpose and satisfaction.

CHAPTER 1

THE LECTURE SERIES

———

It was 7 a.m. when Jaime awoke on Monday morning with the sun shining through the window. He rolled out of bed, turned off his alarm clock, and kissed his wife good morning. As he stepped into his slippers, he moved to the window and looked outside. A beautiful day awaited him—a day he had been preparing for a long while.

He slipped into the shower, washed, and wrapped himself in a robe before shaving the few grey whiskers that emerged from his face. He looked at his reflection through the mirror and stared into his own brown eyes. *It's going to be a great day.*

Jaime dressed himself in his favorite pair of tan slacks and a blue button-up shirt. Grabbing his briefcase, he headed downstairs. His children were still asleep in their rooms as Jaime tiptoed past, trying not to wake them. Quietly, he turned the corner and entered the kitchen, where he toasted two slices of whole-grain bread and spread butter and jam to his liking. His mind raced ahead to the moment when, in a few hours, he would be in front of hundreds of people.

Muttering to himself, he practiced his punch lines while emphasizing pauses and rehearsing hand movements. From one side of the kitchen to the other, he moved, gesturing to an imaginary audience. Footsteps descending the stairs alerted him to his wife coming down to greet him.

"Good morning, honey. Getting ready, are we?" she chuckled.

Jaime smiled. "Just going through a few lines," he said.

"What time does it start?"

"Ten a.m. PACCAR Hall. I should probably get going soon. It's about a twenty-minute walk, and I want to get there early."

"You'll do great," she said.

"Thanks, sweetie. See you this afternoon."

After kissing her forehead, he grabbed his briefcase and headed out the door.

Jaime walked through the U-District of Seattle, passing tall evergreen trees and parks with green lawns, before turning onto University Avenue. Bikers rushed by, and students stormed in and out of bookstores, buying materials for the first day of the spring term.

Jaime reminisced about his time as a college student here many years before. He had lived in an apartment only a few blocks away from campus when he'd been new to college with no real direction in life. Now, many years later, he felt somewhat nostalgic as he once again stepped onto the University of Washington's campus. This time, though, his role would be different.

Despite having walked these grounds for years, Jaime still found himself slightly disorientated and needing to rely on his phone's mapping capabilities to locate his building.

"PACCAR Hall, there it is," he said to himself.

It was only a stone's throw away, so Jaime strutted across campus through the hordes of students and approached the building. He smiled when he saw the university's marketing material about the event that day: "Lecture Series Guest Speaker Jaime Gonzalez, today at 10 a.m., main auditorium."

Jaime checked his watch—9:30 a.m. Plenty of time.

He entered the building and made his way to the designated auditorium. It was a large room with enough chairs to seat close to eight hundred people. All the entry-level business classes like accounting and finance were held in this room, but today the university would use it as the location for their guest speaker to give the first of his multi-week lecture series.

Jaime made his way to the half-moon stage and stepped onto the platform to familiarize himself with his surroundings by walking around. He moved around, waving his hands, speaking under his breath, and rehearsing bits of his first lecture.

A few early students lounged in their seats and chuckled Jaime's antics. Many had their headphones plugged in but couldn't help noticing the strange man talking to himself on stage.

As the clock neared the hour mark, more and more people filled the auditorium. Word of mouth and promotional materials had gained momentum on campus and throughout the city, and Jaime's first ordeal was about to attract an audience of close to three hundred people—some students and others not.

Not bad for day one, Jaime thought as he looked out at the gathering.

Now center stage, he connected his microphone and clipped it to the second button from the top on his shirt. When the clock struck 10 a.m., the auditorium lights dimmed and the stage lights focused on him. The audience hushed each other, and all fell into silence as Jaime cleared his throat, stared into the eyes of his listeners, and began his well-rehearsed introduction.

"Good morning," he began. "My name is Jaime Gonzalez, and it is my honor to have the privilege of presenting this multi-week lecture series to you."

* * *

Some years earlier, a young Jaime seated in the middle row in the PACCAR Hall auditorium looked on stage at the speaker as he finished his presentation on career choices for young business majors.

"In summary," the career advisor concluded, "congratulations on being admitted to the program. From here, you will all need to work hard in your classes and begin attending recruitment opportunities on the side so you can line up a summer internship."

As a new student to the University of Washington's Foster School of Business, Jaime was ecstatic for his next few years of life. However, he felt somewhat lost as to how exactly they would play out when he and the rest of his incoming class attended the lecture on career advice for young professionals.

"Following that," the speaker continued, "you'll finish your senior capstone project, and hopefully you will have a full-time job lined up to begin shortly after graduation. Then you will begin the next stage of your life as a working professional!" She clapped her hands together excitedly as she finished.

It's that easy? he thought.

Jaime glanced around at his fellow students and noted their worried faces. The first day into the program and they all looked like deer in headlights.

The clock struck the hour mark, and the auditorium slowly emptied. Students crammed through the exit doors and eagerly headed to their next appointment.

A friendly face walked up next to Jaime and flicked his arm.

"Hey there, Jaime," he said.

"Hey, Ian," Jaime said, returning the gesture with a friendly shove.

"Some meeting that was," Ian said as they walked out together.

"You can say that again," Jaime replied.

"I don't know about you, but I have no idea what I want to do this summer," Ian added dejectedly.

"Me neither."

"I mean, how am I supposed to compete with everybody else for an internship? You know Caitlyn Hansen is in our class too. Right? She got a perfect score on the entrance exams. Do you have any idea how bad she is gonna make the curve for us?"

Ian's joking tone began to turn frantic. He ran his fingers through his long curly hair as he looked down at the ground in terror. "Oh man, I can see it now. My life is crumbling before me."

Jaime playfully nudged his friend's shoulder. "Okay hey, hey, relax, man. Simmer down. How can you expect a bunch of twenty-year-olds to know what the rest of their lives will look like?"

"By making them decide before they can even think about it," his friend joked. They both laughed.

The two walked down their university halls and observed the flustered faces of some of the other students. It seemed they weren't the only ones stressing.

"I don't like it, man," Jaime confessed, frustrated.

"What?" Ian asked.

"I just feel like sometimes we get treated like robots. We have to do something that we don't even know if we want to do."

"What do you mean?"

"I dunno." Jaime shrugged. "It doesn't feel right. It's just not me." He rubbed his hands against his forehead and took a deep breath. "There must be more than just the options they show us."

"Yeah, I get that," his friend said. "But, what else would you do?"

"Well," Jaime sighed, "I've always loved to travel. I figured I'd find out what I want to do in life by following what I love."

"That's an interesting idea," his friend said. "Never really thought about it that way."

* * *

Years later, Jaime's role in PACCAR Hall had reversed as he now found himself on the same stage delivering a message to a large audience.

"When I was in your shoes some time ago," Jaime said, after introducing himself to the several hundred people in the audience. "I remember being exactly where you are now.

I would frequently look around at all my peers and notice how they all seemed so worried. They felt constant pressure to conform and become a certain kind of person in order to be successful in life. They had to choose a certain career and hobby, have a certain personality, and like certain things. With each decision, they became less and less themselves."

Jaime looked around at the audience and raised his hands toward them as he asked a question. "How many of you out there feel like that somewhat describes your situation?"

A throng of nervous hands shot in the air, followed by united and relieved laughter.

Jaime chuckled with them and continued.

"I was just like you. I also had this feeling of constant pressure to become something I wasn't. Yet, I couldn't help but feel like something was wrong. I had this innate feeling that being different was okay. At the time, I couldn't put an exact word to what I was feeling, but now I see this was the beginning of my discovering the principle of nonconformity."

An audience of bustling students quickly turned into a silent crowd of attentive listeners.

Got 'em, Jaime thought. It appeared his mini rehearsals from the kitchen to an imaginary audience had paid off.

"You might be thinking, 'What exactly is nonconformity?' Well, at its core, nonconformity is being true to yourself. It is choosing to follow your own passions instead of following the crowd. It is awareness of what the world values, deciding if those values align with your own, and then intentionally choosing a path forward. It is a principle of action—choosing who and what you want to be, even if that is different from the norm."

He went on. "I decided at that moment of my life that I wanted to prove I could turn out just fine by choosing to do things differently. I had a passion for traveling the world, and even though it conflicted with the pressures I was experiencing at the time to study, I wasn't afraid not to fit a mold. I decided to follow my passion. I traveled to places around the world, and on these travels, I learned profound lessons that helped shape the rest of my life. From this small desire to be different came a deeper exploration into the principle of nonconformity.

"And so, during my lecture series over the next few weeks, I'm going to share with you five lessons I learned on those trips to help you discover the power of nonconformity and the liberating feeling of going off course. I do hope it will be beneficial in changing your perspective and equipping you with a new mentality to live not just a successful life but, rather, a fulfilling life."

Jaime paused in his walk from one side of the stage to the other. As he began moving again, he saw almost every head in the audience followed his movement.

"My method for teaching these principles will be based on my travels because travel was what first exposed me to the idea of being a nonconformist. However, you don't have to travel the world to be a nonconformist. The principles I will teach in this lecture are applicable to anyone, anywhere in the world.

"Unfortunately, time will not permit us to touch on everything as it pertains to the topic of nonconformity, and besides, I'm afraid much of this topic can only be learned through experience. Nevertheless, at the conclusion of each lecture, I'd like to engage in a brief question and answer to allow for some fun discussion."

The crowd broke out in excited chatter, and Jaime checked the clock. Time to begin.

"With that, I think it's time we get started." Jaime's chest rose as he took a deep breath and began his lecture.

CHAPTER 2

KUWA HURU

The darkness was paralyzing.

Jaime slipped his hands out of his pocket every few steps to warm his fingers. The windchill was far below zero, and he had long since lost feeling in his hands. As he blew warm air and rubbed them together, he tried to get a grip on his surroundings. Dirt, rock, snow, a footpath leading up—still another hour or so, at least.

Jaime's legs seemed at the brink of collapse with each step. The altitude hadn't bothered him so much a few hours ago, but now, he felt as if he was desperately gasping for oxygen through a tiny straw. His pack, though weighing only twenty pounds, pressed down on him like a massive boulder.

He looked up to try and spot the end of the trail, but all he could see was blackness.

"Steph!" he called out. "Taiyu!"

Jaime knew they were only ten or twenty yards away but the thick darkness and powerful wind proved too much for his exhausted voice to reach them.

He checked the time. It was 4:32 a.m. *How long have we been climbing?*

Overwhelmed and exhausted, Jaime sat down. He crept into a small corner where a large boulder shielded him momentarily from the wind and leaned against it. He rubbed his head with his palms and let out a small sigh. His feet ached, his knees were stiff, and his eyes desperately wanted to close.

He fought the urge to fall asleep, but the wind seemed to take all his energy with each subsequent gust. The cold air chilled him down to the bone. To stay warm, he had to keep moving, but he was unable to muster the strength to lift his body and continue upward. Now stuck, he wondered if he would ever make it to the top.

* * *

"I'd like to begin by saying this," Jaime continued as he moved to the center of the half-moon stage. It was about the width of a basketball court and Jaime's figure was the center of attention with the stage lights shining on him.

"Many of you are in a unique stage of life as college students where you can focus entirely on yourselves. You are studying for a future career, you are having fun with your friends, and you are enjoying the young adult phase of your life to the fullest, as you should.

"But face it, you all share a feeling of uncertainty for the future. You don't know where you'll work, what job you'll have, and even where you will be. You don't know much of anything, really," he said, a bit pessimistically.

"I know some of you in this audience are not students, and that's fine. But unless anyone out there has a crystal ball, I think all of us know what it feels like to worry about the future.

"That is why I've chosen this topic for this lesson first. When you decide to live a nonconformist life, you choose opportunity instead of security. You choose to make your own path instead of following someone else's. Like an entrepreneur starting their own business, this will require you to work with a lot of ambiguity and wade through unknown waters. So I would like to begin our course by talking about the first important lesson that comes when one decides to live a nonconformist life—facing fear.

"And to do this, I'd like to invite you to join me on a trip to Mount Kilimanjaro."

* * *

Jaime caught the first glimpse of sunlight from the seat of his international flight to Tanzania. He could see the bright rays creep over the horizon and give light to the wide expanse of African plains. Miles and miles of grasslands covered the earth's surface, and herds of animals clustered together, intermixing peacefully. In the distance, Jaime thought he saw a massive snowcapped mountain coming into view.

The term *The Seven Summits* refers to the seven tallest peaks on the seven continents, and Mount Kilimanjaro claims this honor for Africa at 19,341 feet. Hikers from around the world gather year-round to face this colossal mountain, famous for its breathtaking scenery and its five different climate zones. Though enormous, it is not nearly as dangerous as its counterparts on other continents.

K2, for example, is the second tallest mountain in the world, located in the Karakoram Range to the northeast of the Himalayas, and has a mortality rate of 29 percent. Mount Kilimanjaro's is .03 percent.[4] So while there is certainly some risk involved in summiting the tallest freestanding mountain in the world, Mount Kilimanjaro is more of an adventurous and thrilling experience than it is deadly.

In fact, the mountain is actually quite a popular location for runners. Kenyan marathon athletes are said to be the best runners alive because they supposedly run up and down the mountain for practice.

This aspect—the safe yet adventurous nature of the mountain—called to Jaime.

After landing at the Arusha National Airport, Jaime made his way to a hostel he had found online called *African Paradise*. His room was small, about the same size as his room back home, but it was packed with two bunkbeds and barely enough closet space to put his stuff. Each bed had a white net hanging over it to

---

4 "Is Climbing Kilimanjaro Dangerous?" Climbing Kilimanjaro, accessed November 12, 2020.

protect its guest from an unwanted visit from mosquitoes. Definitely not a five-star resort, but Jaime liked it that way.

While he was getting settled in, another traveler entered the room.

"Hey there, pal," the man said in a thick English accent. He was tall, a little over six feet, and had a warm tone to his voice. "You just getting here?"

"Yeah," Jaime replied. "Just flew in this morning."

"Cool, man. Well, hey, a group of us are sitting out in the main room just chattin' and stuff. You should come out and say hello. I think a group of them just got back from Kilimanjaro. Pretty wild if you ask me, but it sounds like they all made it safely."

"They just climbed Kilimanjaro? They're out in the main room?"

"Yeah, go say hello. I'm Tim, by the way. Cheers, roomie."

"Nice to meet you, Tim! I'm Jaime. I'll see you out there," Jaime said, walking quickly out the door.

As Jaime entered the large living room, he joined a conversation of about seven or so people. Three of them had just returned from climbing Mount Kilimanjaro, and several others listened to their recounting of the climb with interest.

"It was hard, yeah, but you guys could do it," one of them said, the tallest of the three.

"Gotta make sure you have a good guide," said a girl with dark green eyes. "Can't do it without one. The country won't let you."

"And you gotta bring warm jackets," a boy threw in. "I underestimated how chilly it was above ten thousand feet and paid the price for it."

"Sounds easy!" said an Indian girl with long black hair who was listening attentively. "I heard anyone can do it. I'm thinking of signing up tomorrow."

"I wouldn't speak so quickly," the green-eyed girl said. "A lot of people think because Kilimanjaro isn't a glacier that it's a cakewalk. Lots of unprepared people end up paying money for someone to basically carry them up the mountain, and they end up getting into a lot of trouble. If you think this is going to be some sort of walk in the park, you're in for a surprise."

"I'm not worried," the Indian girl retorted. "I've done plenty of hikes back home and should be fine."

Another girl in the circle noticed Jaime's presence and, lifting her eyebrows at him, said, "You look interested. Thinking of climbing?"

"Yeah," Jaime answered. "I'm just looking for a group."

"You're in luck," she said. "It's cheaper if you have at least four, and we are just a group of two. You could tag along with us, and we could do it together if we find one more person. We want to leave in two days."

"Works for me," Jaime said, trying to sound cool but poorly hiding his childish excitement on the inside. "I'm Jaime."

"Jaime, right on. I'm Steph," she said, extending her hand. She was thin, a tad shorter than Jaime, and had curly brown hair draped down her back in a ponytail. Her pretty blue eyes and warm smile emitted a sense of friendliness. "This is Taiyu," she said, pointing to the male to her right. "He's from Japan."

"Nice to meet you, Jaime," Taiyu said cordially. His long black hair was pushed back by his red bandanna, and at just under six feet, he was only slightly taller than Jaime.

"And I'm Shanzee," said the Indian girl as she approached the group. "If you're needing four people for the trip, I hope it's not a burden if I join you?"

"Not at all!" replied Steph. "This is perfect! I'll go ahead and let the climbing company know we have a group, and they should get back to us soon."

"Awesome," Jaime said. "Looks like we'll all be getting to know each other pretty well over the next few days."

* * *

The climbing company van reached the end of a dirt road and dropped off Jaime and his new climbing partners to begin their seven-day ascent of Mount Kilimanjaro. Joining them were two professional guides and a few other porters who were in charge of carrying gear. Fortunately for the first-time climbers, they would only have to worry about carrying a day pack with essentials while the porters heaved up the rest of their clothes and sleeping equipment.

At the beginning of their trek, Jaime was just enjoying getting to know his new friends. Steph and Shanzee, originally from Canada and New Jersey, were both recent college grads and were spending six months traveling before finding work. Taiyu was twenty-six, from Japan, and had just quit his job and was taking a break before transitioning into the finance world as an investment banker. Jaime was the youngest of the bunch at nineteen, but he was stoked to meet people from around the world who, like him, had veered a bit off the common path and had landed themselves in Africa.

They were an unlikely group to begin a hike to the peak of the tallest mountain in Africa. Yet it didn't take long for the four of them to become friends.

"We have to take a picture to signify the beginning of our trip!" said Shanzee.

Taiyu, the photographer of the bunch, rolled his hiker's backpack off his shoulder and fiddled through his stuff until he pulled out his nice camera and asked a passerby to snap a photo of them.

"Let's make sure we get the background in the shot," said Steph.

The four scooted back enough so the snowcapped peak of Mount Kilimanjaro was visible in the distance. Beneath it, the gray rocky slopes cascaded down to the Marula trees, marking the beginning of a new climate zone. Almost twelve thousand feet separated Jaime and his friends from the summit, and they wouldn't return to civilization for another seven days.

They took the photo, and together, the four of them set off into the morning sun to begin their hike. Jaime adjusted his backpack he had borrowed from the hiking company and made sure his hat protected him from the hot sun.

Accompanying the group of four were a pair of guides, Osmani and Prosper. Both were natives of Tanzania and had led trips to the summit over one hundred times.

"Nice to meet you, my friends,'" Osmani said as he extended a hand to each of them. Osmani was the shorter of the two. He had a sharp jawline and a faint mustache. His head was always slightly titled whenever he spoke, and his eyes were captivating. He had a rather scrawny build with extremely thin arms and legs, and one could only wonder how a man of this size was capable of leading trips to the summit of Africa's tallest peak for a living. "I'll be your lead guide for the trip, and Prosper here will be my assistant," he said, pointing to his right.

"That's right, it's no nickname!" Prosper joked. "My mother always knew I was going to prosper in life, so she reminded me of it every day with my name. If you wanna prosper on this trip to the summit, I suggest you follow me!" He let out a loud chuckle, and Jaime immediately felt comfortable around him.

Prosper was the more relaxed of the two. While Osmani had to occupy himself with the logistics of the climb and was more in charge of the group's safety, Prosper assumed the role of the cool, relaxed, humorous guide. His large hiking boots matched his beige cargo pants and blue long sleeve shirt that fit loosely over his somewhat plump build. His favorite red bandanna was dangling about his neck or fitted loosely across his forehead at all times. He kept his beard scraggly and was always asking for spare Snickers bars to keep his hunger at bay.

"So, Osmani, what's our schedule looking like for the next few days?" Steph asked.

"Well, it will take us six days to reach the top of Mount Kili. We will climb anywhere from three to six hours every day. Sometimes flat, sometimes steep, just depends."

"That's it?" Shanzee said. "Sounds kinda slow. Don't you think?"

"And what are we gonna be eating?" Taiyu blurted out.

"The porters will make all your meals, so you won't have to worry about that."

"Very yummy food. They even give you popcorn," Prosper said with a smile.

"Make sure you drink lots of water every day. Dehydration is terrible on Mount Kili," added Osmani.

"Woo-hoo! This is gonna be a blast!" Shanzee said. Her outfit of denim jeans and regular sneakers made her seem a bit unsuited for a hike like this, but her enthusiasm was enough to brush the thought aside. "I've talked to a lot of people about this hike, and they said it's pretty much a breeze."

"Hmph, we'll see. Twenty bucks says Shanzee's the first one to get altitude sickness!" Jaime said, poking fun at his new friend.

"Yeah, yeah. Don't ask me to carry you down when you get tired!" she fired back.

"Let's just hope Taiyu doesn't fall off a cliff trying to get a good shot with his camera," Steph said, as they all laughed.

The group set out on the steady incline and began their seven-day roundtrip journey to the top. Surrounding them was a thick forest with all kinds of wildlife. Africa was known for its impressive diversity of flora and fauna, and Mount Kilimanjaro was one of the best places to see a wide range of ecosystems. Jaime noticed how the mossy branches seemed to have a life of their own as they twisted and turned around vines, roots, and nearby trees. For now, the group would be spared some shade from the trees, but it was still hot enough to keep them sweating.

In between stretches of silence, the group made small talk. They talked about life back home and future plans. Jaime noticed how everyone seemed to follow the beat of their own drum. Taiyu told them about his strict family upbringing and how his parents had always pressured him to pursue a career as a doctor. Feeling overwhelmed by his parents' expectations, he decided to drop out of school and begin a two-year adventure of traveling the world. Spending three months at a time working in Australia would usually provide him with enough money to spend the following six months traveling. He had previously been through much of Southeast Asia before deciding to travel to Africa. He wasn't sure when he would return to Tokyo to finish school, but he was intent on experiencing life now and returning to a good job in finance upon his return.

Shanzee was from the United States and attended college in New Jersey, where she grew up. Africa was the first time she had ever left the country before, and she did it mainly because she didn't know what she wanted to do in life and didn't want to make a decision just yet. She bounced back and forth between majors and hadn't settled on one yet, as many young college students are familiar with, but she was certain she would leave school with a great job that paid well.

Steph had worked most recently as a teller at a local bank in Canada. She was from a small town where people had been living for many generations. Her mom ran a business of her own selling garden supplies that Steph occasionally assisted with, but something about the world excited her and called her to leave her little town and see more. She hadn't gone to college and didn't plan to. She figured she could get by just fine with her street smarts, and traveling would undoubtably help her develop them. This was probably one of the reasons Steph was so much fun to be around. She was very socially aware and always found a way to be friends with whomever she met.

Every forty-five minutes or so, the group would stop to take a break, drink water, and go to the bathroom somewhere in the woods. Jaime was resting in the middle of the road on a walking stick he had picked up along the way when Osmani motioned for him to jump off the path to let people behind him pass. As he skipped to the side, a wave of seven or so African men seemed to whiz by, carrying two enormous bags, which must have weighed forty or fifty pounds each. These men, almost as skinny as Osmani, were simply another breed. With one bag strapped to their backs and the other balanced on their heads, they stormed up the mountain at an incredible pace. Jaime waved at them and smiled in amazement as their bright white teeth smiled back at him. They said, "Jambo!" as they passed. Hello! In the local language of Swahili.

"Those bags must weigh fifty pounds apiece!" Jaime remarked.

"Those are the porters," Osmani said. "For seven dollars a day, those guys carry all the gear up the mountain."

"But they're like twigs!"

"They've done it many times. You get used to it. I used to be a porter too a few years ago before they made me a guide. It's not so bad."

"Why don't they do something a little less intense?" Steph asked.

"They love the mountain. Sure, the pay as a porter isn't great, but after a few years, if you become a guide like me, you do well. I'm very lucky to be where I am."

"Okay, but how on earth do you get used to something like that? I don't think I'd ever be able to last that long," Taiyu said.

"A lot of tasks seem daunting at the beginning," Osmani said. "You just have to take it one step at a time. As a porter, no single step is too hard. You just have to keep moving—one step at a time."

Jaime smiled. *One step at a time.* On a mountain, the phrase seemed to carry a bit more weight.

As more porters rushed by like a stampede of buffalo, Jaime was again amazed at their brute strength. Only seven dollars a day seemed so low for such hard workers. He tried to smile bigger each time they passed to boost their spirits.

The sun began to set as they arrived at their first campsite of the day. The breeze picked up, and the four of them made their way inside the tent where they would have dinner. Jaime stretched his hand to open up the tent before him and ducked his head to enter the relatively small dinner arrangement.

The tent was no bigger than six feet by six feet, with barely enough room for someone to stand upright. Hunched over, Jaime scooted onto the stool around the table that sat four. One of the porters, acting as the waiter tonight, brought in the popcorn as the first course, followed by the best soup Jaime had ever had and a delicious yet simple meal of rice and chicken. The four of them felt a bit spoiled eating a multiple course meal they didn't even help cook on a mountain, but they did their best to express gratitude for the service.

Night fell upon the hikers, and the chatter of other hikers nearby as well as the sound of the jungle were audible from within Jaime's tent. He inched closer to the entrance and unzipped the door, poking his head out just enough to see the night sky. Far away from any light pollution, Jaime could see thousands upon thousands of stars as clear as he'd ever seen. A subtle grin spread over his face, and he thought about the next day as sleep overtook him.

* * *

The next few days were nearly identical. Wakeup call at 7 a.m., breakfast, pack up camp, and begin hiking by around 9 a.m. The scenery had changed from a thick green jungle to nothing but rocks. The dirt path was almost nonexistent now, with soccer-ball-sized stones sprinkled in the way.

In the first few days, the group entertained themselves with get-to-know-you games and trivia, but after hours of playing, boredom started to settle in.

"Okay, Jaime, I got another riddle for you," Steph said, trying to lighten the mood after hours of hiking in the sun. "Forward I'm heavy, backward I'm not. What am I?"

"If you're anything other than a king-size Snickers bar, I really don't care."

"Ah, come on, man! Lighten up!"

"We've been doing riddles for hours! Let's pick a new genre, please."

"Fine," Steph said. "Hey, uh, Prosper! What do you do to pass the time as you hike?"

Prosper spoke up from the back of the group, "Hmm, well, I sing!"

"Get out! You're a singer?" Shanzee said.

"Not a good one, but people have sung a particular song on the mountain for as long as I can remember. It goes like this."

Prosper's deep voice began to sing a light tune:

Jambo! Jambo bwana!
Habari gani? Mzuri sana!
Wageni, mwakaribishwa!
Kilimanjaro? Hakuna Matata!
Tembea pole pole. Hakuna Matata!
Utafika Uhuru. Hakuna Matata!

"Pretty cool!" Jaime said. "What does it mean?"

"It's a conversation," Prosper said. "It starts by saying, 'Hello, how are you?' and then the person responds saying, 'Good.' Then it goes on to say, 'Welcome. Come see Kilimanjaro. No worries! Take it slow there, friend. No worries. See you at the top, hakuna matata!'"

"You mean 'hakuna matata' actually means 'no worries'?"

"That's right, rafiki, which also means friend."

"You're kidding," Jaime said. "Hey Shanzee, you hear that? *Lion King* actually had it right!"

Shanzee didn't respond.

"She fell back a while ago," said Prosper. "Osmani is with her. We'll see her tonight at camp."

Jaime, Steph, and Taiyu exchanged a nervous glance but continued. Jaime hoped she was okay. He couldn't help but think about what Shanzee had said at the beginning of the trip. *Anyone can climb Kilimanjaro.*

* * *

It was night now, and Shanzee had made it to the campsite several hours after the rest of the group. She had immediately collapsed in her tent to rest, but Osmani had called an important meeting to plan for the next day.

"Tomorrow, we will begin our summit push," he began. "Shanzee, you'll leave with me at midnight. The rest of you will leave at 1 a.m. so we can all make it to the summit at the same time for the best part—sunrise."

Everyone nodded in agreement. Shanzee seemed worried, and Jaime walked over to her.

"Hey, hakuna matata," he said. "You're gonna make it."

"I hope. I'm so tired."

"Remember, one step at a time." Jaime smiled.

"Yeah, right."

Jaime lay in his tent again that night, wondering what it would be like to reach the summit. It was odd to be trying to sleep around 7 p.m., but even that early bedtime would only give him six hours of sleep.

* * *

Darkness.

The wind was roaring when they began their hike. Jaime zipped up his puffer coat, pulled up his liner pants on top of his sweats, and pulled the strings on each of his black ski gloves to tighten their grip around his wrists. Taiyu and Steph were equally as puffy with layer after layer to combat the biting cold. They were beginning the summit push at sixteen thousand feet, and temperatures could drop below zero with the wind chill. With Osmani and Shanzee already gone an hour earlier, Prosper led the way as each member followed in a single-file line up the slope to the summit.

Their path was composed of countless switchbacks and blistering wind, and the altitude made their feet feel like they had bowling balls attached to them. Jaime had to go incredibly slowly. He would raise his feet to take a step, stop for a breath, and then continue with the next step. Each step seemed harder than the last as he quickly lost feeling in his toes, but he tried to get into a rhythm—step, breathe, step.

The dark night enveloped them the whole way, leaving them feeling completely isolated while only being a few feet apart.

"Steph, Taiyu!" Jaime called out.

Jaime sat down behind the largest rock he could find to protect him from the wind. His energy was leaving him, and he had no idea how much was left on the hike. He was cold, hungry, and bitter.

This is stupid, he thought. *Why am I even doing this?*

As he sat there sulking in his own frustration, Osmani's words from earlier that week fluttered into his mind.

A lot of tasks seem daunting at the beginning. You just have to take it one step at a time. No single step is too hard.

One step at a time.

"Ugh, fine!" Jaime shouted to himself. *I can't see the end, but at least I can see what's in front of me.*

Bracing himself against the rock, he slowly raised himself to his feet and took a deep breath of air. The cold air entered his lungs, and with it came a wave of energy. The blood returned to his fingers and hands, and in a flash, he felt a surge in spirit that he hadn't experienced all morning.

One foot after the other, Jaime continued climbing. "Step, breathe, step," he told himself—one at a time.

With each additional inch forward, Jaime could see more of the path in front of him unfold. He was gaining momentum now. Step, breathe, step. His boots seemed to stick firmly into the ground and launch him farther each step. He felt like he was moving faster than he had ever gone before. It was as if he'd entered some kind of trance. Time disappeared entirely, and all Jaime could focus on was the moment right before him, the next step.

Suddenly, several figures emerged in the distance. The darkness slowly dissipated, and Jaime could now make out the faint silhouettes of Steph, Taiyu, and Shanzee. Whew, she made it!

The three of them stood next to a sign that Jaime recognized as the landmark, indicating the summit was only a few hundred yards away.

Another figure emerged from behind the sign, and Jaime quickly recognized Osmani's voice: "Just thirty more minutes to the top! We are almost there!" he cried through the wind.

Reaching the end of the incline and approaching the small slope toward the mountain's summit, Jaime turned back for the first time during that morning's hike. What he saw took his breath away.

In the distance, he could see the African horizon begin to change colors into a purplish pink blend as the sun began to rise. With the increase of light, he could see the vast and endless African plains begin to take shape. The faint purplish-gray of the sun's morning rays broke through across the horizon. *Was this behind me the whole time?*

Jaime took in the beauty for a moment and remembered he had only a few yards left in his journey. After an easy trek across the now snow-covered path, Jaime finally reached a circular opening about the size of a basketball court and realized where he was standing.

The summit of Mount Kilimanjaro.

Taiyu, Steph, and Shanzee pulled Jaime into a giant bear hug. They squeezed so hard Jaime could barely breathe.

"We did it!" Taiyu exclaimed.

"Okay, okay, I get! Can you let me breathe now!"

"Not yet, I'm still cold!" joked Steph.

Released from the hug, Jaime looked at his surroundings. Though his group was one of the first to reach the summit that morning, the relatively flat mountain peak already had nearly fifty people celebrating their ascent and taking pictures next to the famous alluring green sign that said, "Congratulations, you are now at Uhuru Peak!"

Behind the sign, Jaime could see the entirety of the path he had taken to get to the top. He saw where the dirt path became snow; he spotted the location where he had stopped unexpectedly and doubted himself. From this perspective, he could now see where the trail took him even though he couldn't in the moment. The beauty before him was more than he ever imagined. It was all worth it.

"Uhuru Peak," said Prosper, who had snuck up next to him. "You know what 'uhuru' means?"

"No, I guess not."

"Freedom," he whispered. "This is Freedom Peak. It's quite liberating to look back on the path and see how far you've come, even when you didn't know how it would end. It makes you feel like you can keep finding new paths with new destinations."

Jaime pondered those words for a moment. "That's beautiful," he said.

Prosper eyed Jaime and then gently removed a beautifully colored bracelet from his wrist. "Here, keep this," Prosper said, extending the gift to Jaime. "My father gave me this bracelet when I was young and finding my way, and it has since joined me on all of my life's adventure. Something tells me you are doing the same. I hope this bracelet will be a token of the beginning of that journey for you."

Jaime received the bracelet and was touched. "Prosper, thank you so much."

"Kuwa Huru, my friend. Kuwa Huru. It's something we say here."

"What does it mean?" Jaime asked.

"Be free," Prosper whispered.

He gave Jaime a warm congratulatory smile and then walked away.

Jaime smiled, gripping his new bracelet tightly, and took a deep breath. For some reason, the air didn't feel so thin anymore.

* * *

Jaime stopped, and with a pause, he began wrapping up the first lecture of his series.

"As you can see," he said, "the biggest takeaway for me from Mount Kilimanjaro was about fear. I didn't know what to expect from the climb to the summit. In the dark, I had no idea where I was going. Now I'd like to connect how this relates to nonconformity.

"In life, there will be pressure to know what your future will look. The expectation will be to have a five-, ten-, even thirty-year plan with details about where you'll be and what job position you'll have. I'm not saying, this is bad; in fact, planning ahead is a really good thing. But as we make our life plans, we also need to keep in mind that plans change. It's nice to think that our life course will always go according to plan, but more often than not, life will probably lead us on a course where we will sometimes have to wander in the dark.

"The nonconformist is okay with uncertainty. The nonconformist takes life one step at a time, even if they can only see right in front of them. The person who chooses to conform will choose only those paths whose destinations are known and guaranteed. They are afraid of veering off the path, so they stick to what is safe, secure, and visible. Nonconformists, on the other hand, are not afraid to try a new course because they know this will lead to new discoveries. They know what Kuwa Huru means because they feel free to pursue whatever path their dreams lead them on. It takes bravery, but as I learned on Kilimanjaro, it will be worth it.

"Now, I'm sure there are questions about that experience, and I'd like to open it up to the audience for some comments."

A few hands shot in the air. A girl in the third row from the front raised her hand, and Jaime called on her.

"Hi there. One thing I wanted to ask was about the summit push. You said you left in the middle of the night and the darkness made that part difficult for you. Why couldn't you have just gone during the day when it was light out? Wouldn't that have been easier?"

"Great question. Yes, we could have left in the morning and hiked with the sun, which would have removed many difficulties that arose from climbing in the dark. However, there would be one caveat. The most enjoyable and beautiful part of reaching the summit is seeing the sunrise from the top, and if you don't leave when it's dark, you'll miss that experience. Climbing during the day would still give you a pretty view, but it's not the same. In life, it's often similar. If you want to get the best result, you'll probably have to face some hard obstacles that others won't, and those will definitely test your grit. In the end, you won't just end up with a better view. You'll have grown so much more from that experience. You learn to humbly appreciate your trials."

"You don't think it would have been nice to see the sunset instead?"

"Sure, that would have been great, but then you face a whole new set of challenges. Climbing down in the dark is much more dangerous than climbing up because slipping going downhill is much more punishing. Hiking during the middle of the day when it's the hottest will force you to bring more water, making your load heavier. So, to some degree, you do have to pick your battles. There will rarely ever be an easy route to success, and anyone who tells you otherwise is trying to sell you something."

Another question from a girl in the back sparked Jaime's curiosity. "My name is Rachel. I think while one could view taking the unbeaten path approach as fun and exciting, others may view it as irresponsible and unprepared. How would you respond to that?"

Jaime stroked his chin and thought about his response for a moment. It was a fantastic question. "Well, I certainly don't want to argue that there is a singular correct answer to your question," he began. "There are benefits of both approaches, no doubt. Have a look at what Phil Knight, the founder of Nike, said about this."

Jaime clicked a button, and the projector displayed a single quote.

"There comes a time in every life when the past recedes, and the future opens. It's that moment when you turn to face the unknown. Some will turn back to what they already know. Some will walk straight ahead into uncertainty. I can't tell you which one is right. But I can tell you which one is more fun."

—PHILIP H. KNIGHT[5]

"So, I guess I have to agree with Phil Knight here. I'm not saying that it's bad to take the popular route or choose the most common career. If that's what you want to do, then do that! However, if you are only choosing that path because you are afraid to choose something else, I think you have something to learn here. Having plans or goals is certainly a good thing because, without them, you are selling yourself short. Though how exactly you arrive at that goal—and all the little details in between—well, you just can't predict those. Too many factors are simply out of your control. All you can do is take it one step at a time. So, is that irresponsible? I don't think so. I think it is a balance. The only way to plan and be prepared for every possible detail in life is to become completely withdrawn from it."

The audience fell silent. Jaime looked at the clock and noticed their hour session was nearing its close. *Not bad for the first lecture,* he thought.

"Well, I hope you all enjoyed today's lesson as I think it sets the tone for the rest of our time together," Jaime said as students

---

5   "Phil Knight Quotes," AZ Quotes, accessed November 23, 2020.

began to pack up their belongings. "I look forward to meeting you next week when we will look at another powerful lesson I learned from a much larger mountain with which you are probably more familiar. Until then, Kuwa Huru!"

CHAPTER 3

GODDESS OF THE SKY

―

This is it. I'm going to die.

Jaime's mind could barely cope with the reality surrounding him. He pressed his forehead to the window by his seat and looked outside.

It was hailing. The small bullet-like pellets pounded mercilessly on the old plane's cabin, making loud cracking sounds, and Jaime felt like he was taking heavy fire in the middle of a warzone. His seat shook from beneath him with the plane's every movement, and every other moment the knot in his stomach felt like he was dropping one hundred feet on a carnival ride.

Moments earlier, it had been a smooth flight from Kathmandu's International Airport. Jaime had been able to see the luscious green mountains forming the wide canyon that seemed only an arm's reach away. Now, however, he saw nothing but white fog. A terrible storm had engulfed the aircraft and swallowed all aboard into a nightmare.

It was a smaller plane, at least twenty years old or so and fitting thirty people at most. A single aisle ran down the middle with one seat on each side, and the walls seemed to be some flimsy, cheap metal. Its small frame shook vehemently in the storm, and Jaime couldn't tell if the turbulence or the terrifying thought he might die in this very moment made him sick to his stomach.

"I can't see anything!" Carol screamed from the seat next to him. She tried leaning over Jaime to catch a glimpse of land through the window but saw only a white oblivion.

"I can't either!" Jaime yelled back. "It's all clouds. We must be in the middle of it!"

He whipped his head around to look at the other passengers on board. They were all in a state of shock, even the locals. One older woman clung to her two small children and pressed her japamala, Buddhist prayer beads, to her lips as she whispered a silent plea to a higher power with her eyes closed.

God help us, Jaime thought.

He sat back in his seat and looked at Carol. She had lifted her feet to her seat and hugged her knees to her chest. She swayed back and forth, eyes closed, and tears streaming down her cheeks as she pretended it was all just a dream.

Jaime leaned over to comfort his friend. "It's okay, Carol," he said, trying to conceal his own fear. "Everything is going to be all right."

She cried silently, terrified, refusing to believe it was real. Her nails dug into her pants as she waited for nature to decide her fate.

The forty-five-minute flight from takeoff to touch down seemed to stretch on into eternity. Worse yet, the destination was the Lukla airport, notoriously known as the number one most dangerous airport in the world. Now, in the thick of the storm and barraged by the elements, Jaime didn't doubt it.

Suddenly, a strong whip of lightning pierced the sky. The plane shook harder than ever before and took a plunge into the canyon. They were going down. Passengers screamed. The pilots frantically pushed buttons, flipped switches, and struggled to get in touch with the Lukla airport staff to no avail.

Jaime wrapped his arms around Carol and tried to comfort her. Outside, the chaos ensued. Jaime closed his eyes and tried to pretend he was somewhere else. He wanted to fall asleep and pretend it was all a dream. Very slowly, he began drifting into unconsciousness.

Suddenly, it appeared.

"Jaime, look!" Carol cried.

Jaime opened his eyes and immediately saw it.

A runway.

"Are you seeing what I'm seeing?" Carol said startled. "It looks like, like it's—"

"Slanted?" Jaime finished.

Nestled beneath them in the middle of the mountains was the Lukla Airport runway. In what was the only possible way to fit a long enough runway into the mountainous landscape, architects had decided to build the landing strip into the slope of the mountain, using the decline to help departing flights catch speed to take off and the incline to help arriving flights slow down.

Magnificent as it was, Lukla had a history of airplane crashes over the years, and flying in a storm only increased those unfortunate odds.

The pilots managed to gain temporary control of the plane to position it for landing, but they were descending fast. Too fast.

"Oh my gosh," Carol said, realizing their predicament. "We're coming in fast. We don't have time to adjust. We're going to crash!"

Jaime took one last gaze out the window and knew it was true. He could see the plane's odd angle of entry into the mountainside. The pilots fought to pull up, but it was useless. They were about to add their names to the list of victims to the world's most dangerous airport.

Jaime and Carol gripped each other and closed their eyes as they prepared to make contact. This was it.

There was a brief moment, a space in time before the plane touched the ground, when everything seemed at peace, like the blissful calm before the storm.

And then a powerful thud.

* * *

Feet shuffled and chairs creaked as students made their way into the large PACCAR Hall auditorium. A week had gone by since Jaime last entered the large room, and now he made his way to the center of the stage and greeted his audience.

"It's good to see you all here again," he said as he addressed the crowd. He was glad to see an auditorium that looked slightly larger than the week before.

"Some years ago," he began, "I was in an auditorium just like this one. It was my graduation ceremony, and all my peers had gathered to listen to our commencement speech. The speaker was an older man, an entrepreneur, I think, and he said something life changing that I'd like to talk about today."

As he spoke to the audience, Jaime's mind flashed back to that moment as a soon-to-be graduate. He felt as if he was reliving it for the first time.

"If I've learned one thing in my career," the speaker said, "it's that success is not a finite resource."

Jaime remembered tilting his head to one side, confused.

"Guys," the speaker continued, "I'm going to tell you something you might not understand now, but I hope one day you will."

He paused.

"If I could say one thing tonight, it's this. There's plenty of room at the top. Extend your hand to lift those around you, even if it means they might end up on the same plane or higher."

The audience was quiet, clearly a bit surprised by the peculiar advice. It seemed a bit contradictory.

Interesting advice, Jaime remembered thinking at the time

Snapping back to the present, he continued addressing the crowd. "I wish I could have understood the wisdom behind those words when I first heard them, but unfortunately, I wasn't ready. I didn't believe what the speaker said because it went against everything I learned as a business student, and I couldn't see how it made any sense. Luckily, I remembered his words on one of my adventures, and I have since never been able to forget them."

The audience shifted in their seats, anxious to hear what came next.

"So instead of in this auditorium," Jaime said with a sweep of his hands, "I'd like you to imagine yourself somewhere much farther away, surrounded by mountains, yaks, and snow. Today, you will join me in learning something from the highest point on earth—Mount Everest."

* * *

At the end of April Jaime found himself sitting in a foreign airport by himself with only a backpack and duffle bag. A voice over the intercom spoke in a foreign language as he watched passengers hustle by in an effort to make their flights. The men wore long tunic-like gowns of simple colors, and nearly all the woman wore hijabs that covered their entire head and rested gently along their necks and shoulders. Behind him, a sign reminded a jet-lagged Jaime of his current location at Abu Dhabi International Airport.

He raised his palms to his head and rubbed his eyes before using his thumbs to massage his temples. He was accustomed to sleep deprivation after just finishing another year of college, but jetlag was a different beast.

The things I do for cheap flights, he thought.

His itinerary was brutal—LAX to Kathmandu with a seventeen-hour layover in the United Arab Emirates. The first leg had been long, but the layover killed him. He had landed at around 7 p.m. local time, and his flight wasn't until noon the next day.

He had tossed around the idea of getting a rental car and zooming off to Ferrari Land, a touristic attraction in Dubai not more than two hours away. But the time of night and the additional cost of renting a car and paying the park admission fee was enough to keep him rooted to the airport.

Instead of nice leather seats in a Ferrari, I'm in a not-so-nice leather seat in the airport, he moped.

Jaime tried to sleep as much as he could over the next twenty-four hours to help the time pass by faster. After another long plane ride to Kathmandu and an eternal line at immigrations, he finally exited the busy airport and stepped outside to hail a taxi. Dozens of locals awaited the new arrivals and competed to attract a customer to their cab. Jaime kept to the side and crept through a crowd of tourists as he singled out a cab away from the chaos.

"I'm going to the Hostel Himalaya," Jaime told his taxi driver. "Do you know it?"

"Yes, Hostel Himalaya. Yes, I know it. Two thousand Rupees," the driver said.

"How about one thousand?" Jaime countered.

"Okay, no problem. Let's go," the driver responded without any hesitation or need for argument.

That was easy, Jaime thought.

As the driver sped away from the cluster of tourists and taxistas, Jaime gazed out his window at the new city before him.

Dust was everywhere.

Kathmandu was crowded and busy. In Tanzania, on Jaime's last trip, the African plains seemed endless, stretching farther than the eye could see. Space was no scarce resource.

Kathmandu, on the other hand, could not have been more opposite.

The bustling, congested, and dusty city boasted apartment buildings made of brick that stood over fifteen stories high.

Debris flew every which way on the poorly paved roads as pedestrians covered the streets and sidewalks like a flustered colony of ants.

Perhaps the most horrifying sight was the traffic system. Cars did whatever they wanted. There were no lines on the roads, no signs (that anyone paid attention to, anyway), no stoplights; everything was just one single street with vehicles fighting to get where they needed to go. Jaime learned quickly from his taxi ride that driving in Nepal was nothing like driving back home.

Once in the city, it only took Jaime a few moments to realize his driver had no idea where he was going. Every few minutes, he tilted his head to the side as he looked in his rearview mirror and asked in a thick Nepali accent, "What was name of the hotel?" When Jaime repeated his destination, the driver would nod his head reassuringly and reply, "Oh yes, Hostel Himalaya. Yes, I know it. Almost there." It wouldn't take long for Jaime to catch the driver glancing at him through the mirror again, his head tilted to one side, repeating the process.

At one intersection, he asked to see a picture of the hostel logo and again affirmed that he knew the place well. Jaime wondered if he should get out and find another taxi, but he decided not to. As lost as the taxi driver seemed, he made good conversation and was helpful in explaining more about the city of Kathmandu.

"Kathmandu very big, many people. People here are very poor, yes, very poor. But we live good lives and are very grateful."

Jaime felt his stomach growl. "What's the best food here?"

"The typical food in Nepal is dal bhat. Good plate, steamed rice and cooked lentils. Very typical. Then you must also try the momos."

"Momos?"

"I think you call them something… dumplings! Steamed dumplings! Yes, very tasty. Many good places to try. You must try."

"That's great. Thanks for the recommendation." Jaime returned to the view outside his window and noticed the faint outline of a mountain range in the distance.

"Those are the Himalayas?" Jaime asked.

"Yes, yes," he said. "Mountains here are very sacred for us. We see them as goddesses of Mother Nature. I have never been myself, but lots of you people go. Very expensive for us but beautiful mountains."

He paused as he turned his head and looked briefly at the mountain range before returning his eyes to the road. He sighed.

"We used to be able to see the Himalayas better from here, but because of climate change, they are slowly disappearing."

Returning his gaze to the city around him, Jaime felt overwhelmed. So many cars, so many people. The infrastructure was so old. He had never seen a place so cramped or congested. It was so different from his expectation of a clean, fresh, and green city next to the mountains. It made him all the more anxious to begin his hike.

When Jaime had nearly given up hope, the driver took an unexpected turn down a random alley. Sure enough, as they pulled in, Jaime saw a sign atop a building that read, "Welcome to Hostel Himalaya."

"We are here. It was nice to meet you, my friend. Namaste."

"Thank you!" Jaime replied as he handed the man his change. "Wait, what does 'namaste' mean?"

"It is a greeting we say here. It literally means 'the divine in me recognizes the divine in you.' We say it whenever we say hello or goodbye."

"Oh, cool," he remarked. "Well, namaste to you too!" Jaime shouted as he stepped out of the car.

Jaime flung his backpack over his shoulder and looked at the structure before him. Hostel Himalaya—a rather cool place for a college student's budget. The three-story building was surrounded by a well-meaning attempt at a garden. It was squeezed in between several other buildings, apparently apartments, and didn't cover much ground.

As Jaime entered the hostel lobby, he heard a rumble of footsteps coming down the stairs. Turning the corner and locking eyes with him was a familiar face.

"Jaime! You made it, mate!" the girl said as he sprinted toward him and jumped into his arms.

"Carol! You're here already!" Jaime said as he returned the friendly hug.

"Yep, flight got in yesterday!" she said. "How was the trip?"

"Long, and I'm exhausted but ready to get climbing!" he exclaimed.

Carol was slightly taller than Jaime with a slender figure and long black hair. She wore the loose-fitting elephant pants common to tourists in Southeast Asia, a tank top, and a pair of flip flops. A childhood friend of Jaime's, Carol and her family moved back to Australia when her dad got a new job working for the government. The two stayed in touch and had fantasized about going on a subsequent trip together to Mount Everest.

The original idea was to summit. However, after doing some research and realizing they would need between thirty and one hundred and fifty thousand dollars to hire a guiding company, they figured a hike to the base camp would be a sufficient blend of entertainment, frugality, and safety. An eighty-mile round trip hike reaching altitudes as high as 18,400 feet, the Everest Base Camp (EBC) trek provides travelers with a cost-sensitive alternative to climbing the mountain while allowing them to experience the awe of the Himalayas. One highlight of the hike is to climb a nearby peak, Kala Patthar, which gives the iconic panorama view of the Himalayas and a breathtaking vista of Mount Everest.

"Man, it's so great to see you!" Jaime said.

"You too, mate. Can't believe we are actually doing this!" she responded.

"I know, crazy. Right? Let's hope we both make it back alive," Jaime joked.

"I got our flights booked to Lukla, the airport we have to fly into from Kathmandu to begin our trek. We can go into town today to buy some last-minute things if you need them. Otherwise, we should probably hit the sack early tonight and rest up."

"Yeah, right," Jaime agreed. "Was your flight here okay?"

"Long, but yeah. Had a long layover in Sydney, but I slept most of the way on the plane."

"That's good. Hey, have you met people who have already done it?"

"Yeah, a few of the people staying here have been. They said it's lovely. We won't need a guide, it seems, and all the inns along the way have plenty of space."

"That's good to hear," Jaime muttered. "I can't say I would be excited to sleep outside in just my sleeping bag."

"Yeah, don't worry. We'll be fine. Better get settled in here, though, mate. Our flight leaves tomorrow!"

Ugh, please, Jaime thought, *not another airplane ride.*

***

Solid ground had never felt so good.

Jaime and Carol's plane had miraculously landed safely at Lukla's airport, though the abrupt and powerful thud of the airplane hitting the runway had left Jaime with a kink in his neck.

After stepping off the aircraft, he and Carol both plopped themselves onto the ground and lay there momentarily, grateful to still be alive.

"Remind me never to do that again," Carol huffed as she rolled onto her back in a patch of grass.

"So, I shouldn't remind you that we still have to fly out of here," Jaime chuckled and then sat up and grabbed his backpack. "Come on. Let's get going."

Grabbing her note pad, Carol reviewed the itinerary she had jotted down a few days prior. "So, it's going to be a twelve-day round trip," she said. "We stop at an inn each day, so we won't have to worry about setting up camp or anything. The last one is called Gorak Shep, where we'll stay for a night, see the base camp, and then climb up the nearby peak called Kala Patthar to get the iconic panorama of Everest and the Himalayas."

"Can't wait," Jaime said, elated.

"Food gets more expensive as we go up, and we'll be able to fill up water and make sure it's clean using the iodine tablets we bought in town," she added.

"It's not going to get too cold, either," Jaime added. "I checked the weather, and it looks like we will be climbing in forty-degree weather during the day if the sun is out. It will get cold at night, but we should be fine as long as we are inside."

"Right then," Carol said, as she pointed her hand toward a path that was at the edge of town. "This place is tiny, and that looks like the start of the trail over there. Let's get going!"

The pair made their way to the entrance of the Everest Base Camp (EBC) trek, which wasn't really much of an entrance at all. Jaime thought such a famous location would feature large signs or dramatic banners, but the entrance to the trail was only a simple archway with a stone statue on either side.

"Well, here we go!" Jaime exclaimed.

When people think of the Himalayas and Mount Everest, they probably think of blizzards, snow-covered mountains, and insane windstorms. While true in the winter, the spring season in the Himalayas is different. Hikers begin the climb to EBC at around ten thousand feet, and in the spring, the snow melts at that altitude. The scenery of the early parts of their hike was much like what Jaime was used to from his hikes in the Pacific Northwest with thick forest, the smell of fresh mountain air, and the sound of running water. Jaime felt at home.

This made for a relatively easy ascent. The pair didn't have to wear any heavy clothing while they hiked; Jaime was in a long sleeve shirt, a pair of shorts, and Nike running shoes while Carol sported a pair of athletic shorts and a tank top.

Jaime led the way with Carol following right behind. Their path followed a series of dirt trails along the sides of mountains followed by numerous long suspension bridges that connected two mountains in a canyon. Walking across each bridge made Jaime feel like he was in a *Lord of the Rings* movie, and at any second, one of his feet would slip through the mossy wood to send him crashing down into the icy river below.

As they traversed another one-hundred-yard bridge crossing, Jaime was halfway through when, up ahead, Carol spotted an unexpected roadblock.

"Uh, Jaime!" she yelled as her voice echoed in the canyon.

"What?" he shouted back.

"I think we need to turn around!" she cried.

"Turn around?" he responded, confused. "Why?"

"Because a herd of yaks is walking right at us!" Her voice was a mixture of amazement and terror.

Jaime abandoned his focus on the few feet in front of him and lifted his head to look down the bridge. Up ahead, a pack of yaks were already on the bridge and walking across directly at him.

Jaime had never seen a yak before. He froze in awe of these massive creatures as they slowly moved in his direction. They had thick bushy hair converging at their underside and large horns like those of a bull protruding from the tops of their heads. Behind them, a local Nepali herder nudged the pack along with a stick and loud grunts.

Even though the yaks were moving slowly, Jaime quickly realized if he didn't get out of their way fast, he would get firsthand experience of the power of a yak's horns. He quickly turned around and retraced his steps with Carol to avoid being pushed off the edge.

Once back on the mountainside, Carol motioned her hands toward the mountain's slope.

"Make sure you always stand uphill from them!" Carol shouted from a few meters away. "I read it in a review online. You don't want to be the unlucky bloke who gets pushed off a hill by a grumpy yak!"

"Yeah, right." Jaime gulped as he grabbed on to a nearby tree to move off the path momentarily.

After four hours of climbing, Carol and Jaime were ahead of schedule and reached the hostel where they would settle in for the night in a town called Namche.

"Ah, Namche," Jaime said. "The last city before it's just hostels."

"What do you mean, mate?" Carol asked.

"After here, it will only be one or two hostels at each place we stop. This is our last chance to buy any gear we forget, books, and decent tasting food. From then on, it's gonna feel pretty deserted."

"So you're saying this is my last chance to get a donut," she relented.

"Exactly." Jaime laughed.

The two strolled through Namche and looked at the different coffee shops and supply stores that filled the small town. Namche was an enormous amphitheater-like city that rested in the nook of the mountain. Thousand-foot drop-offs surrounded the city at its lowest points, and just across the canyon travelers got a glimpse of a behemoth mountain face that cascaded down into the river. Jaime and Carol chose a coffee shop with a great view of the mountain to have hot chocolate and bread.

As they ate, someone barged into the restaurant and whispered something to the shop owner, who immediately looked somber. The owners mumbled words to each other. Something had clearly happened.

"Another death up at the summit," a neighboring customer told Jaime.

"You heard too?" Jaime asked, turning toward him.

"Word travels fast on the mountain," he replied.

"How did he die?" Carol added.

"Altitude sickness, I heard. It can get anyone."

"I thought if you acclimatize right, you wouldn't get altitude sickness?" Jaime questioned.

"No one is bigger than the mountain," he responded, very matter-of-factly. "You can acclimatize all you want, but in the end, the human body isn't meant to survive at those heights."

"Oh," Carol concluded. "Maybe it wasn't such a bad thing that we couldn't go to the summit."

"Yeah, maybe not," Jaime nodded.

"Keep your wits about you down here too," the man said. "The Trek to Base Camp has claimed plenty of lives on its own."

The man stood up and left the small cafe. Jaime and Carol looked at each other and shuddered.

"When we got past the flight to Lukla," Carol said, "I thought that it was pretty safe sailing from there."

"Yeah, me too," Jaime agreed. He sipped a bit of his hot chocolate. "Don't worry, as long as we keep an eye out for each other, we'll be okay."

Carol nodded and nibbled on the last piece of bread. All of a sudden, the reality of death on the mountain sank in a bit deeper for both of them. This was no joke.

* * *

The climb up to Mount Everest was very different from Jaime's climb up Mount Kilimanjaro in that, since there were only two of them this time, the hours they spent climbing were mostly silent. For four hours each day, they would hike several yards away from each other and focus entirely on their breathing. This, combined with the perfect temperature, turned out to be one of Jaime's more therapeutic hikes.

Upon arriving at the next stop of hostels, they grabbed a room and spent the evening having dinner and playing card games with other travelers on the same trek. It was a helpful way to pass the time, and Jaime loved meeting and learning about the lives of other travelers who, like him, had also ventured off course in life and somehow found their way into a small hostel in the middle of the largest mountain range in the world.

After several days of this routine, Jaime and Carol finally found themselves at Gorak Shep, the last hostel before Everest Base Camp and conveniently positioned right at the base of Kala Patthar, where they would see the iconic view of Mother Nature's highest point on earth. They downed another serving of dal bhat and then played cards with new friends.

"Another round of hearts?" Jaime asked as he shuffled the deck.

"Sure," a good-humored Irishman named John replied. "No cheating this time, though."

"If you're not cheating, you're not trying hard enough!" Jaime joked. Carol moaned as she rolled her eyes at him.

"Only joking." He grinned.

As Jaime dealt out another round of hearts, a girl name Silvia asked, "I wonder what it would be like to summit Everest nowadays."

"How do you mean?" replied Carol.

"I don't know. I just keep reading these articles about how Everest is getting more crowded every year. Anybody with money can basically pay their way to the top without really earning it."

"Yeah, I heard that too," John said. "You see that picture of the huge queue just to stand at the summit? The line was like two hours long."

"No way," Jaime exclaimed in shock.

"Some guy coming down told me he only had a few seconds at the top, and it was ruined by people shoving and trying to get their selfie. There just wasn't enough room for everyone up there."

"I hope it's not too cramped when we get to the top of Kala Patthar," said Carol.

Silvia sipped her coffee as the crew fell silent. Jaime finished shuffling, and they tried to distract themselves with another round of hearts.

* * *

At 4 a.m. in the black of night, Jaime and Carol were bound up in their warmest clothing as they stood at the base of Kala Patthar, anxious to summit by sunrise.

"It's about two hours to the top," Jaime said, standing at the base, "and it's pretty steep the whole way. The top of this is almost nineteen thousand feet, so don't rush. Let's just get into our rhythm like we've done all trip, and it should be fine."

"Got it," Carol said.

Carrying only a day pack, Jaime felt tired with every step, but he was used to the altitude by now. Mount Kilimanjaro had helped his lungs feel familiar at high altitudes, and he had learned the secret to proper ascents. "Step, breath, step," he told himself. "Step, breath, step." Occasionally, he thought he could do fine without following his pattern, but eventually, he ended up kicking himself because he had to catch his breath. Just stick to your pattern. Focus.

Carol fell behind a little every now and then due to fighting a nagging hip injury, but the two pushed on. As Jaime would occasionally peer over his shoulder to check on her, he noticed a few other climbers had begun their ascent. He remembered their conversation the night prior and didn't want a rushed experience at the summit. He wanted time to admire the mountain range.

As the first sign of light crept over the mountains, the world around them grew brighter with each passing minute. Almost without noticing, Jaime and Carol soon found themselves just beneath the summit of Kala Patthar. After a few final steps together, the two stood atop the peak, turned around, and gazed into the enormous face of Mount Everest.

"You know," Carol began, breathing heavily between words, "in Nepal, Everest was given several names by the locals to honor her immensity and grandeur. They had a feeling of humility and submissiveness to the mountain, believing it was somehow connected to a higher power. They gave her names like Chomolungma or Sagarmatha."

"What does that mean?" Jaime panted. He could see his breath with each exhale.

"Goddess of the Sky," Carol replied.

"Fitting," Jaime conceded. "It's so massive. I've never seen anything like this."

"Yeah. It makes you feel pretty small. Doesn't it, mate?"

"Yeah, it really does."

Carol walked a few steps away by herself and knelt down on a rock to write in her journal. Jaime kept his eyes fixed on the mountain. He sat down and felt as if he was an old sherpa villager discovering this peak for the first time.

I can understand the reverence, he thought, overwhelmed at the mountain's size.

Something about being in the presence of such a massive figure made him acutely aware of his nothingness in the universe.

We are so small in the world, Jaime thought.

Peace overtook him. He closed his eyes and imagined himself floating outside of his body and observing the setting. He saw himself at the peak. He saw Carol alone nearby. He saw the ice rock and the glaciers below. His mind climbed higher and higher into the sky, and the outline of him and Carol faded away. All he could see now was an enormous mountain that dwarfed its surroundings.

Jaime's nothingness became more real to him than ever before. He felt so vulnerable, so small, so... equal to everyone else.

It felt good.

I guess it's nice to feel small every once in a while, he thought.

Bringing him back to the moment, a fellow traveler approached the summit, clearly exhausted. He was bear-crawling up, with all fours against the slope and his head facing down. When he neared the top, he raised his head and saw Jaime and Carol standing above him on the mountain's peak. He stopped immediately with a hesitant look on his face.

Without thinking, Jaime reached his hand down and offered it to the stranger.

"Here, take my hand!" he said as he pulled him up to the summit to share it with Carol.

"Thank you!" the stranger gasped. "I didn't want to intrude on your space up here."

"Ah, no worries. There's plenty of room at the top!" Jaime said instinctively.

He froze.

The words came out so naturally. Jaime didn't really think when he said it. Suddenly, Jaime's mind flashed back to the moment when he first heard that phrase:

"There's plenty of room at the top," the speaker said. "Never hesitate to reach a helping hand to those around you, even if it means they might end up higher than you."

At that moment, Jaime finally understood the wisdom behind those words.

There's more to life than just getting to the top, he thought. *It's about helping others to get there too.*

Carol came to Jaime's side, and in her puffy coat, she wrapped her arms around her friend. "We did it, mate. We did it."

"Yeah, we did," he said.

"And I got one heck of a picture of you daydreaming while staring at that summit!"

Jaime smiled.

Each with one arm around the other, they sat there for a moment in silence and observed the beauty around them. A profound sense of humility entered Jaime's heart.

He would never be the same.

As the last bit of sun emerged from the east behind Everest's peak, Jaime gave silent thanks to the mountain.

* * *

Back in PACCAR Hall, Jaime made his final remarks.

"I only learned the meaning behind the words of that wise businessman after my trip to Everest. There's plenty of room at the top. It requires a tremendous amount of effort to achieve success and not become arrogant or prideful. Only a humble man will want to share his success with his fellow man, and only by reaching out to help him can we do that."

An introspective pause allowed Jaime to continue.

"The world will tell you, as it told me, that in order to be successful, you must beat out the person next to you; that in order to achieve success, you must take it, steal it, hold on to it, do whatever you can to prevent the man next to you from attaining it. This world encourages us to become self-centered. This is a trap.

"Nonconformity taught me to disbelieve this idea. From Everest, I learned success is not a finite resource; it grows as it is shared. I now believe humility and service are just as much an integral part of success as determination and competition.

"You see, something about Everest was special for me. Only when I saw how small I was in the world did I realize how pathetic it was to think I was better than anyone else. When we realize our nothingness, we can't hide from the truth that we are all nothing. Thus we are all equals. This profound sense of humility naturally carries us to care for our fellow man, no matter who they are. We can't help but instinctively reach out and extend a hand to help them in their journey. As one hand lifts another, both are elevated."

After pausing, Jaime pointed to the outstretched hand of a student in a dark blue shirt.

"Mr. Gonzalez, I see what you're saying, but I see some potential problems. For me, I've always had a hard time finding the balance between humility and confidence. It seems that whenever I focus on being humble, I don't feel confident, and when I feel confident, I get cocky. Where's the balance?"

"Great question," Jaime said. "I've definitely felt that way, and my experience at Everest certainly caused me to think about that."

He raised his head to the ceiling and slowly walked from one side of the stage to the other, stroking his chin as he left the audience in silence.

"I think when it comes down to it, the key to balancing confidence and humility is gratitude," he said. "If you pat yourself on the back because you're being such a great guy, you're failing to recognize the things around you that contributed to your success. You will get caught in a selfish cycle of feeding your ego that will ultimately end in your own downfall."

"Um, I'm not sure I understand, sir," the young man responded.

Jaime went on. "Some of the best athletes I know are the most humble. They give credit to their teammates after a great win, and they say 'we' instead of 'me.' Likewise, in Christianity, for example, followers are taught that by placing their entire trust in a perfect deity, it allows them to remain in humble awe of their nothingness in comparison to their God while at the same time feeling empowered with a confidence that with Him they can do anything.

"On the contrary," he continued, "the shelves of libraries around the world are filled with stories of prideful protagonists who make themselves their own God and go about their lives seeking nothing but their own praise. History will show you time and time again how they end up falling victim to their own hubris."

Another hand shot up. "There is a lot of truth, though, to your thoughts about it being a dog-eat-dog world," a shorter male said from the corner of the room. "If you help somebody up, or you don't go out and take what you want, it's likely others might beat you to your goal."

"Sure, and I think there might be some truth to that," Jaime conceded. "But it is also a silly idea based on the assumption that somebody else's success diminishes your own worth, which is certainly not true. Reaching out to help another person will not put you at risk. The irony of life is that as you seek to serve those around you, you wind up being the greatest benefactor of your service. But you can never get your true intentions mixed up. If you reach out half-heartedly, people will see right through you."

Jaime checked his watch and noticed their time together was nearing its end.

"I'll see you all again next week when we review another important lesson that resulted from my nonconformist approach to life."

The students stood up, slung their backpacks over their shoulders, and made their way out the rows.

"You may want to have a map handy next time to be able to locate the next country that will teach us this lesson," he called after them with a grin. "You've probably never heard of it before."

CHAPTER 4

ISLES OF THE SEA

"Grab it! Grab it!"

"I can't. I can't!" Jaime yelled. "It keeps getting away!"

"Stop being such a baby and just grab it!" Winston said, laughing and poking fun at Jaime. Tarawa, Peter, and a few of the kids watched nearby, laughing along as well.

Jaime took a deep breath and bent over again in the knee-deep water. The ocean reef provided his prey with some protection, but Jaime had been able to pry it out using the tools Peter had lent him. Now, as his prize was completely exposed, all Jaime had to do was grab it out of the water.

"Get it! Get it before it goes back into a hole!" Winston cried, almost in tears now from laughing so hard.

"It's not funny, okay! It's harder than it looks!"

"It's not gonna bite you. Just grab it!"

Jaime followed his prey a few feet until it slowed to a momentary stop. Then he shot his hands into the water at lightning speed and seized the aquatic invertebrate. It was small enough to fit mostly inside his hands. He could feel the slimy, sticky creature squirm as he pulled it out of the water.

"Nice work! Okay, now you have to find its head and bite down hard!"

"What? Bite its head?"

"Yes, hurry!"

Jaime looked down at the slimy creature. Its tentacles swirled all over the place and latched on over its head to protect itself from its enemy. Jaime pried the tentacles apart, but each time another took its place. A dark black ink started to ooze from the creature's center and landed on Jaime's swimsuit, leaving inky spots.

"I can't find it!" Jaime yelled. "It's too slimy!"

"There it is! You got it! Do it now! Bite!"

Jaime took a deep breath. He tried to summon all his courage but then let out a yell.

"Ahhhhh!" he cried as he targeted the octopus's head and clamped down hard.

Immediately, it went limp.

"Yeah! I did it!" Jaime exclaimed.

"Woo-hoo!" Winston exclaimed. "Lunch is served!"

* * *

The audience hushed as their speaker made his way to center stage. Grabbing the mic and addressing his crowd, Jaime spoke.

"Good morning! I hope you all had a good week and are excited for another lecture today. It's nice to see more of you here than last week."

He glanced across the room and noticed not only more students but more adults. It seemed his lectures had attracted more faculty and parents as well.

"I hope you have enjoyed the course so far. We have traveled to Africa, Nepal, and as I said last week, you might need a map to see where we will be traveling to today."

He paused again, as he often practiced at home before his presentations.

"The lesson we will learn today will be a powerful and important one for all of you. It seems we are all living in a world that is as polarized as ever, and something must be done to counter this.

"My hope is when you walk out those auditorium doors today and resume your normal lives, you will take with you at least a piece of what I learned from a distant place, somewhere in the Pacific, in the isles of the sea.

* * *

About four thousand miles to the west of California's coast exists a completely different world.

The Southeast Pacific is unlike any other place on earth. With dozens of languages spoken across hundreds of little islands, this region is home to numerous countries whose culture varies drastically from that of the modern world. The sound of cars bustling through a city is replaced with the sound of the waves, encouraging the inhabitants to slow down and enjoy life at a peaceful pace.

Many sailors voyaging across the Pacific Ocean have landed on some of these islands and become familiar with what is termed "the island culture." Characterized by unparalleled charity and hospitality, the people who live in this part of the world are unlike anything most people will ever meet.

Kiribati (pronounced "Kiri - bas") is one of these countries. With a population of just over one hundred thousand people, Kiribati is only accessible via flights from Fiji and other small islands in the area. It spans over 1.3 million square miles and is one of the only countries in the world to cover all four hemispheres.[6] Most of the country's thirty-two islands are actually atolls—long thin strips of land that curve in the

---

6   *Encyclopedia Britannica*, s.v. "Kiribati," accessed November 20, 2020.

shape of a C and create a shallow bay with bright blue water on one side and deep ocean blue on the other.

South Tarawa, the country's main atoll, is the largest of these and holds most of the population. Stretching over ten miles long and only 1,500 feet wide, South Tarawa's highest elevation is only ten feet above sea level, giving the country some fame across the world for being at risk of sinking due to global warming.[7]

This unique, away-from-the-world element of Kiribati attracted Jaime. His best friend and roommate from his freshman year of college, Winston, had been living in Kiribati for the last few years as a volunteer. He had once sent Jaime pictures of his setup in Kiribati and told him about some of his experiences with the culture. The world away from the world had some kind of magnetic pull on Jaime, and he knew he had to visit.

* * *

The summer after his second year in college, Jaime stepped foot into the small, crowded customs room and shortly after made it outside to the passenger pick-up area. Out of the corner of his eye, he spotted a familiar face.

"Jaime!" a friendly voice yelled.

Standing on top of a stone platform that supported the iron-sheeted roof was Winston. He was hanging off the post like a sailor looking off into the sea, with his free hand holding on to his backpack around his shoulder. His normally tan skin was burned red from the Pacific sun, and the skin around his eyes was peeling.

"Thought you weren't gonna make it," he said, jumping off the stone platform and landing next to Jaime. "Who knows how many more flights those airplanes have in 'em," Winston joked, eyeing the old, overused aircraft.

---

7 *Encyclopedia Britannica*, s.v. "Tarawa," accessed November 20, 2020.

"Not funny," Jaime said, unable to hold back a grin. "You can make those jokes when we get back home."

Jaime reached out a hand to greet his friend, but Winston had already wrapped his arms around Jaime.

"You really missed me, huh?" Jaime said. "Thought you weren't much of a hugger."

"Yeah, it's not really an option down here. You'll see," Winston responded. He led Jaime out of the small airport and through a crowd of people waiting for friends and relatives.

As they walked, Winston asked, "How you been, brother? How's life back home?"

"Good, good, nothing too crazy. Just another year of school finished. How's your gap year been?" Jaime asked.

"You have no idea, man," Winston said. "Life here is unreal. Here, you're about to meet the mom of the family I've been staying with, and you'll see what I mean."

Winston led Jaime toward what had to be a red nineties Suzuki that had seen its fair share of dinks and introduced the woman who emerged from the driver's side door. She was short, about five feet tall, with a colorful flowered skirt and flip-flops. Her white shirt contrasted with her dark islander skin.

"This is Teebora," he said fondly. "She's been taking care of me."

Jaime extended his hand and said, "Nice to meet—"

Teebora ignored it and wrapped her arms around Jaime, squeezing him tightly and planting a kiss on his right cheek.

"Hi. We are so happy you've come to Kiribati," she said in accented English. "I don't speak great English, but I can understand a lot."

"No, no, your English is great," Jaime responded quickly. "Nice to meet you too." He was a bit taken aback by the somewhat uncomfortable crossing of social norms. He noticed Winston behind her laughing under his breath and mouthing "told you" to him.

"Thanks so much for letting me stay with you," Jaime added.

"No problem," she said as she waved her hand like it was nothing. "Come, come. Let's get to the house. Everyone is excited to meet you."

The three of them jumped into the car and left the parking lot. Kiribati was a very thin island with only a single paved road running north and south. At its widest point only a few hundred feet separated the road and the ocean. Houses made of sticks, coconut leaves, concrete, and other random pieces of debris filled the space. Motorcycles weaved around cars like ant colonies, and Jaime was amazed to see such a crowded place in a country he had never previously known.

"This is the main island of Kiribati, Tarawa," Teebora said. "Lots of people."

"I had no idea," Jaime said. "How long have you lived here?"

"My whole life. My kids and I all live here. My kids went to Fiji for school for a few years, but when they finished, they all came back. We live together in my home now. My husband lives here too, but he is on another island for work."

Jaime admired the coconut trees surrounding them, and through an opening ahead, he saw the land converge to a point until only a single bridge, two lanes wide, was visible. Jaime looked on either side of the narrow road and saw a bright shade of blue.

"Is that . . . ?"

"The ocean? Yes," Teebora said. "In some places, the land is only wide enough for the road."

"Beautiful, right?" Winston said, pointing to the bright transparent ocean, blue on both sides of the road.

"I've never seen anything like it," Jaime said, completely stunned. He sat in silence as he observed his surroundings. "The ocean is just right there."

"You won't see water that blue in even the Caribbean," Winston said. "This is only a taste of it, though. In a few days, we are going to an outer island where it's going to be even more remote."

"An outer island?" Jaime asked.

"Yeah, only accessible by flights out of Tarawa. They are literally hundreds of miles away from here with no electricity, cars, or really anything you're used to. I was out there for two months at the beginning of my trip, and I figured you'd want to see it."

"Sounds awesome," Jaime said.

"Yeah, you'll see. For now, enjoy the main island."

Jaime continued to look outside his window in silence, amazed at his first exposure to the island until the old Suzuki pulled in to Teebora's house. As they parked, Jaime stepped outside and noticed the ground was unstable. Sand, he realized. This whole island is a beach. They built their home on sand.

As Teebora motioned them inside, Jaime grabbed his only piece of luggage, a traveler's backpack stashed with clothes, a few snacks (chocolate wasn't found anywhere in Kiribati), and a book to keep him busy during long layovers.

Teebora welcomed Winston and Jaime into her three-bedroom home. Built with cement walls and a wood ceiling, the rooms had tiles with no carpeting. For Kiribati, this was one of the nice homes. There was only one bed in the entire house of seven members because most people grew up sleeping on the ground with only a straw-woven mat and a blanket. It was nothing like what Jaime was used to, yet he felt surprisingly comfortable. The warm, friendly island culture vibes were as tangible as the ocean breeze blowing through the windows.

"The bathroom is over here if you need it," Teebora said, turning to Jaime. "Your room will be done by tonight."

"My room?" Jaime asked.

"Yes, dear, of course, that's what they are building outside!"

Jaime whipped his head around to see three people working on a small hut-like structure. "Those two small boys are my two sons helping our neighbor put everything together."

Jaime was confused. *Are they building that for me?*

"But I don't understand," he said. "I'll only be here for a few days."

"Doesn't matter! We want you to be comfortable," Teebora went on, cutting him off with a grin.

The structure was a hut elevated three feet off the ground, large enough to fit a king-size mattress inside and able to stand upright. It was only a few meters from the house and just a few more from the ocean. Jaime didn't know what to say.

"But the materials, the wood... how did you get everything to make it?"

"We had an old chicken coup that we weren't using anymore, so we just took most of the supplies from that, bought a plastic top for the roof, and then asked our boys to help put it together. It's nothing, really. Don't worry. We are glad to have you."

"But you didn't have to do that! I would be fine sleeping on the floor!" Jaime remarked. A knot started to form in his stomach. He felt guilty they had spent so much time to accommodate him.

"Bahh!" Teebora gawked as she tilted her head slightly back and waved her hand at him. "You and Winston are our guests!"

"It's true," Winston chimed in. "They made me the one next to yours." Just a few meters away from Jaime's future hut was another similar structure that Winston had stayed in for the week he was there before Jaime. "It's just the culture, man. It's what they do here."

These people don't even know me, Jaime thought. He wasn't sure how many people back home would do this for him, yet Teebora and her family seemed to do it without a second thought.

"My kids should be here tonight. They want to play games," Teebora said. "Winston, when are you leaving for Nikunau?"

"In three days."

"Okay. We'll take care of you until then."

* * *

Winston introduced Jaime to the rest of the family that night. Teebora had five kids—two boys and three girls. Her husband had been doing work with the government on Christmas Island and had been gone for the last six months, so Jaime worried about Teebora raising her kids alone. After seeing the kids finish building Jaime's room, prepare and clean up dinner alone, and build a fire to play games, he wasn't too concerned; they seemed like they could manage.

"In Kiribati," Manoa, Teebora's seventeen-year-old daughter, said, "we play Sorry. It's a board game. You know it?"

"Yeah," Jaime said, "Yeah, I think I've played it a few times."

"Not like them," Winston chimed in. "They are next level."

Manoa unrolled the cloth piece and laid it in the center. She sat cross-legged on the ground and draped her long flowered patterned skirt over her legs. The skirts are very popular in island culture and have many names, but in Kiribati they called them "Te Beis (Teh-bays)." Monoa had dark skin and puffy cheeks, and her black, Rapunzel-length hair dangled to her side.

"You can be on my team," Naomi said. "We'll play Winston and my little sister. I never lose," she said with a wink. She had beautiful hair like her sister and was also sitting cross-legged.

Completely barefoot and with no makeup, Naomi's natural beauty was captivating.

It was a simple board game. Using cards, a player and partner advanced a piece around a board until it returned home. Once all pieces were back, that team wins. Jaime had played before, but not with quite as much enthusiasm as Monoa and Naomi. Their brothers, Nooa and Teerute, were also behind them watching, and together, the entire family seemed to erupt in laughter every few seconds. They laughed at mistakes, at jokes, and how Jaime had to keep adjusting his legs from the pain of sitting cross-legged for so long. They laughed at Winston for losing. They laughed at everything, but there was no maliciousness behind their humor. They just couldn't stop laughing.

Jaime had never seen such a display of emotion. In Kiribati, they lived and interacted with strangers differently. It didn't matter that they had only met earlier that day. Jaime felt like he had known them forever.

Lying in adjacent huts later that night, Jaime and Winston stayed up talking as the ocean's waves crashed onto the shore a few meters away. Three days on the main island with Teebora and her family had passed in a flash. Volleyball, spearfishing, cooking local meals—all Jaime could really remember was the beautiful sound of laughter.

"We leave tomorrow for Nikunau," Winston mumbled.

"Can't wait," Jaime said as he lay awake, his head perched just outside of his hut so he could see the stars through the coconut trees above. "What's it like?"

"It's one of the farthest islands away from the main island. Kind of like here, but more primitive. The only houses are stick huts." Winston yawned. "Flights only go once a week. Sometimes, though, they get canceled because of weather or problems with the plane, and if that happens, you wait."

"For how long?"

"A week, until the next plane comes," Winston answered.

"So what you're saying is that if we go, we could get stuck out on a remote island in the middle of the Pacific Ocean with no electricity, no phone service, no money, and no real assurance of when we could come back?"

"Yep."

"Great," Jaime said. "That doesn't worry me at all."

"We'll be fine, man. There is so much to learn out here from these people. Nikunau will be different from anything you've ever seen. And plus, worst case, we could ibobosi."

"Ibobosi?"

"Yeah, it's what you say here when you really need a favor. It's a plea of some sort. If you're desperate and need help, and you tell someone ibobosi, that person will feel a strong obligation to help. It's a bit of a shame to turn down an ibobosi, just because everyone knows you only use them on rare, rare occasions. I think it could work."

"You think so?" Jaime was skeptical. Fulfilling a hefty favor for a complete stranger was not as simple as uttering a single word back home.

"One of the guys who works for the airline is my friend, so maybe."

It was risky, but Jaime knew he had to. Something about the island culture called him deeper.

"Let's do it," he said.

* * *

Jaime pressed his forehead to the window and found himself flying through a blue expanse. He looked out into the horizon as far as he could and couldn't identify where the ocean ended and the sky began. With no clouds, everything was just a beautiful shade of blue.

He peered forward to the front of the plane, and for the first time in over an hour, he saw the outline of an island.

"That's Nikunau," Winston said. "We are almost there."

The plane began its descent and drew close to the land. Jaime's old seat rumbled beneath him like an earthquake as every bit of turbulence could be felt. When Jaime saw what they would be landing on, he gulped nervously.

The unpaved runway wasn't pure sand like he had expected. A single stretch of yellow in the middle of a forest of green trees, it was more like the top of a reef, like someone had cut down all the trees and swept off all the sand to uncover a flat rock surface suitable enough for landing a plane.

This is the strangest runway I've ever seen, Jaime thought. Memories of the Lukla airport and the slanted runway in the Himalayas flashed in his mind. *Maybe not.* He shuddered.

"I got to Kiribati almost a year ago, and it's been about that long since I've been here," Winston said reminiscing.

As they stepped off the rusty aircraft, a throng of people gathered to greet their old friend. Locals immediately swarmed Winston. They hugged him, kissed him, and put flowers over his neck. Winston reciprocated as if a local himself. To Jaime's surprise, the crowd then turned to him and repeated the greeting, squeezing him, cheering, and placing flower necklaces over his neck. The intense hugging from strangers and intrusion of personal space was once again a bit alarming but not a total surprise. *This is how they greet a stranger,* Jaime thought, as he remembered the first time Teebora met him and promptly burst his personal bubble with a kiss on the cheek.

"You used to it by now?" Winston asked.

"Getting there," Jaime said sarcastically as he braced himself for another wave of hugs.

Jaime smiled and hugged each person he met, amazed at how happy they seemed to see him. There were about ten people receiving the two travelers, and leading them was a motherly figure with thick, curly hair that hung down to her waist. She had dark skin with freckles on both sides of her nose, a beautiful smile despite missing a few teeth, and deepness to her brown eyes.

"This is Tarawa," Winston said, motioning toward her. "She's named after the main island, so it will be easy to remember."

"Hello," she said slowly and with a smile.

"No one here really speaks any English, so I'll do my best to translate for you," Winston said.

A few other locals stepped off the plane, and everyone watched as the aircraft took off again and headed back to the main island. Jaime noticed that many people had stuck around just to watch the plane arrive and depart like it was entertainment in itself. *Let's hope it makes it back here in a week*, Jaime thought, as he remembered the likelihood of canceled flights.

"So, where are we staying?" Jaime asked, laughing to himself as he realized they had planned a trip to a remote island without really knowing exactly where they would be sleeping.

"Some American missionaries live on the island and are friends with Tarawa. They are back on the main island for a week, so they said we could stay in their house," Winston replied.

"Their hut, you mean."

"Right," Winston chuckled.

The crowd of locals began to disperse, and Jaime saw groups of three or four stack on to little motorcycles and head off on a dirt path northward. Tarawa had let Winston borrow their motorcycle so they could carry their stuff back to their place, opting to walk with the rest of her family and friends who had come to greet their guests.

Behind Winston on the motorcycle, they road ten minutes down a single road that split Nikunau in half, just like on the main island. They passed huts on both sides of the road. All were elevated a few feet off the ground to protect from bugs and high tide. Every once in a while, they passed large sanctuaries that acted as meeting spots for tribes. The roofs were steep barn-like ceilings that stopped just three feet short of the ground. These structures had no doors. They were open all around the perimeter, so all one had to do was duck down beneath the straw-covered ceiling, and they would be standing inside of a large meeting hall.

At many properties, designated by sticks or rocks acting as borders, Jaime noticed men and women sitting on rocks and using a machete to hack away at individual coconuts. Using the blade to open and cut them in half, the villagers would drain the water from the coconut, storing it in containers for later use. They would then peel the white inner lining of the coconut and save it as food. Finally, they would lay out each half of the coconut with the inside facing the sun and allow it to dry out.

"What are they drying the coconut shells for?" Jaime asked.

"It's the island's source of income," Winston explained. "They can sell the dried coconut shells to cargo ships every so often when they come by, and in exchange, they can buy supplies from them like food, gas, or other things they might need."

"What else do they use the money for?"

"Nothing really," Winston replied. "Apart from buying life-essential items, money doesn't really matter here."

Jaime nodded and continued observing the island. Unlike an atoll, Nikunau was an actual island. Most of the island's population lived on the north and south ends, with about five miles separating them. Jaime could see the ocean about one hundred meters to his right and a thick forest with coconut trees all over on his left. There were no buildings, no coffee shops, no gas stations. It was as primitive a world as Jaime could ever imagine.

A few moments later, the motorcycle slowed to a stop. "We're here," Winston said as they pulled up to a stick hut like the ones Jaime had seen on the way over.

"Home sweet home. This is where we'll crash for a few days. Tarawa said she'd be here in a little bit and we'll have lunch."

"Sweet. I could go for some food right now," Jaime said. "What's on the menu?"

"The menu, every day, will be rice and whatever we catch from the ocean."

"Whatever we catch?" Jaime said, confused.

Winston turned and looked at him with a grin.

***

"Just do it! Do it now! Bite it!"

Jaime clenched his teeth around the head of the octopus and bit down hard. He felt a crunch like he was biting a piece of cartilage from a chicken leg, and suddenly the octopus went limp.

"Good job," Tarawa's husband, Peter, said. It was about the only English words he could say.

"That was awesome," Winston said.

"Most exhilarating thing I've ever done in my life," Jaime bragged.

"Come on," Winston said, as he gave Jaime a congratulatory pat on the back. "Let's head back to the campsite."

The group made their way back the three hundred yards to their campsite. Tarawa and Peter had insisted on taking them to the other side of the island to set up a tarp and canopy where they could enjoy a different beach, fish, and play volleyball. Since Jaime had considered sleeping in a stick hut almost the same thing as camping, this new scenery hardly felt any different.

The last few days on the island had gone by in a flash. They had fished, played volleyball, taken care of tasks around the house, and ridden the motorcycle around the island. Jaime never knew what day of the week it was, and nobody really seemed to care. The sun rose as normal, the temperature was always the same, and with the exception of Sunday when everyone would gather for religious services, every day was basically the same too. For Jaime, it neared boredom, but for the island people who didn't know anything different, every day was bliss.

Today, though, Tarawa had planned for a special ride around the island on the community's only truck. The ride would be about an hour long and would take them to a small lake in the middle of the island. Joining them would be Tarawa's family, including three others that Jaime had met earlier that week.

Edeveen was their three-year-old daughter, and Seguine was the five-year-old boy named after an American missionary. The final member of their home was an old woman named Ngaan. Ngaan was from the north end of Nikunau, and she was mute. She couldn't speak or communicate with anyone, and her family forced her to leave when she was a teenager. One day Tarawa and Peter saw her walking down the road, going hut to hut asking for food. They took her in, fed her, and accepted her into their family as one of their own.

They drove to the north and arrived at the lake, where Peter took Edeveen and Seguine to jump in. Jaime leaned over to Winston and, trying to hide his conversation, asked, "How did they get this truck to show us around, anyway?"

"They paid for it," Winston replied.

"I thought you said they didn't have a lot of money."

"They don't," Winston repeated.

"So, why did they pay for this?"

"You've seen how people are here. Money and material things don't matter to them. Their relationships are everything."

Jaime leaned against the truck as he watched Peter splash around in the lake. "It's just so different than what we're used to."

"It's like I said back on the main island. It's a whole different world out here, and we've got a lot to learn from it," Winston replied.

The family made their way back to the truck and got on. As they drove away, Winston suddenly remembered.

"The lady who schedules flights is close to this spot. Let's swing by and make sure our flight will be coming tomorrow."

Tarawa nodded and informed the driver to make a brief stop on the way home. Moments later, Winston and Jaime jumped off the bed of the truck and approached a local woman in her stick hut a few meters off the road. She was sitting cross-legged around a small campfire-like stove as she heated tea.

Winston began to speak Kiribati to the woman who grabbed the island's only satellite phone and dialed the airline. After a few moments, Jaime could quickly tell that something was off. The woman was shaking her head in sympathy as she spoke to Winston.

"Please, you have to ask for a plane. We have to get back to the main island," Winston said in Kiribati. "Please, if we miss our flight, we will be stuck in Kiribati for a long time. Isn't there anything you can do?"

The woman continued speaking with a dejected look on her face. Winston turned to Jaime and filled him in. "She says she is sorry but that there's nothing she can do. Not enough flights were booked for the way here, so the airline decided to wait until next week."

Jaime's eyes widened. "That would be bad. We'd miss the flight home from the main island. There has to be something she can do. Anything."

Winston's eyes dropped to the ground. He paced back and forth as the lady held the phone to her ears and burst out into a string of Kiribati. She paused for a moment, apparently listening to the other side's response, and then lowered the phone and shook her head at Winston.

Discouraged but not defeated, Winston let out a final series of words in Kiribati, and Jaime thought he recognized one of them.

The lady sighed and put the phone back to her ear. She started speaking fast again, but this time the demeanor in her face changed. She no longer seemed to be fighting a hopeless battle. Though Jaime couldn't understand nearly anything the woman was saying, he managed to make out a single word that changed the course of the entire conversation—ibobosi.

She hung up the phone. "Be at the runway at six a.m. tomorrow."

* * *

Their last dinner with Tarawa and her family was special. Peter had killed one of the four pigs they had, usually saved for special occasions, and cooked it for a farewell meal. Meat was a delicacy in all of Kiribati, and extremely rare in a place like Nikunau. To Jaime, it seemed like it was the best he had ever tasted.

They enjoyed the evening between broken English and the little Kiribati that Jaime had learned and were laughing. After dinner, Jaime and Winston stayed up talking in their hut.

"I didn't expect this when I came here," Jaime said.

"What do you mean?" Winston asked, smacking a mosquito on his leg.

"I've just never seen people give so freely, and to strangers."

"Yeah," Winston agreed.

"We come from different races, different worlds, and I honestly felt sorry for them for their living circumstances. Now, I realize I had it all backward. I think they should feel sorry for us. They seem ten times happier."

"Yeah, I guess that's just how people are here. They just know how to take care of each other."

At 6 a.m. the next morning, a small crowd gathered again to see the plane land on the reef runway. Tarawa had come with her family as well as several of her friends who had joined for camping and enjoyed their visitors. The plane touched down and opened its doors to passengers, and Winston and Jaime took one last moment to take pictures and say goodbye.

"Come back and visit Nikunau," Tarawa told them. "We will be here waiting for you." A tear streamed down her face.

"Thank you for everything," Jaime said. "Korapa."

She bowed her head and gave him a hug. The two turned their backs and waved as they boarded their plane.

They sat in silence as they looked out their window with Nikunau in the distance. It had only been a week, yet Jaime felt like he had lived another life on the remote island. Coming back to the real world wouldn't and couldn't be the same.

They would only spend a few days on the main island before returning to the states. Teebora was there to take care of them again, as both Winston and Jaime suffered from boils and a stomach illness they had caught somewhere on the island. Jaime was sure it had come from the octopus.

They visited a local high school in the area run by the community church and got the internet password in exchange for a few of Jaime's chocolate candies. Some kind of conference was going on at the school, a training of some sort on self-reliance led by leaders from other countries. The boys found a spot in the shade against the building's stone wall where they checked their emails and caught up on a few messages from back home. Lying there, sick and exhausted, the two of them looked like a mess.

A stranger dressed in slacks, a white shirt, and tie passed by the duo as he was apparently leaving a meeting. He looked like he was somebody important. "Man, you guys look wasted. Everything okay?" His voice hinted that he was from either New Zealand or Australia.

"Yeah, we're okay, thanks for asking. Just a little sick," Winston replied.

"Just a little," Jaime said, feigning a smile behind his pale green face.

"Not to worry, mate," he said. "Let me see what I've got for you inside."

Mate, Jaime said to himself. *Man, I miss Carol.*

A few minutes later the man returned. "Here's a bottle of water for each of you and a bottle of orange juice to share to get the Vitamin C up. If you're sick, you might want to take these pills. Now, I'd give you the stronger ones I have in my flat, but my wife thought I shouldn't be walking around giving out strong painkillers to strangers, so you'll have to settle for these ones. But if I'm being honest, a few of these guys and you'll get knocked out anyway."

"Thank you so much," Winston said, reaching his hand out to receive the supplies.

"My wife and I are off to another conference, but if you'd like, you're welcome to hop in our room just over there. We have

AC, Wi-Fi, a comfy couch, and more water and OJ if you'd like it. Let me know if there is anything else I can do."

Winston shot a glance at Jaime and tossed him a bottle of water. They both laughed in disbelief.

"Cheers, mate," Winston said, extending his bottle as a toast.

"Cheers," Jaime croaked. "To Kiribati."

* * *

The audience was quiet as Jaime finished his story.

"'I think the lesson I learned in Kiribati is obvious and powerful," Jaime said as he glanced around at the crowd.

"I was from a different continent. I came from a different culture, a different social class. Everything about me was different from these people. We were total strangers in every aspect. And yet, never in my life have I been treated with such love and generosity than from my friends in Kiribati.

"Today, you will be encouraged to make friends with those who are easy to be friends with, and you will associate with people who are similar to you. The temptation will be there to avoid, even look down on, people who have a different skin color than you, support a different political party than you, or simply dress differently than you. And if you find yourself in this position, beware; life inside a bubble is an empty one.

"Living a nonconformist life and following my passions to travel and see different cultures taught me an important lesson about life that I would not have discovered otherwise. It taught me that we don't have to know each other to show love. We don't need to have everything in common to be friends. We don't even need to speak the same language. We simply need to learn from the people in Kiribati. Show love to a stranger, and your life will be rich."

As Jaime concluded his summary, he gave the usual time to answer a question or two. Only a single hand shot up from the front row.

"Mr. Gonzalez" the girl said quietly, "I get why we should love those around us. It makes sense. But, I mean, sometimes it's hard to love people who are different than you." The girl slumped in her chair, a bit embarrassed to have made such a public, yet genuine, confession.

Jaime gave an empathetic nod. "It is indeed," he said. He thought before he answered. "But if you only love those who are easy to love, you live a very shallow life. You will be doing what everybody else does, and isn't being different from the crowd the very essence of nonconformity?"

"I suppose," she replied. "But I guess it's just easy to be afraid in those kinds of situations."

"Fear and love will always conflict. But I hope our lesson on Kilimanjaro can remind you that being courageous in the face of fear will yield big dividends."

The crowd remained quiet, and Jaime didn't see another hand. He checked his watch and saw that another week's lecture was up.

"Thank you all again for coming," Jaime added. "It's great to see more of you joining us each week. Until next time!"

CHAPTER 5

WAVES

Alicia gripped tightly to her boyfriend's torso, sitting behind him on their rented motorcycle as they road along Carretera 21. It had been a long semester away from her sweetheart of six years, and a two-week vacation in Costa Rica's famous Tamarindo was just what they needed.

A thought occurred, and Alicia leaned forward and put her mouth close to her boyfriend's ear.

"Can I try again?" she asked.

He smiled, turned on his blinker, and pulled over to the shoulder. "Okay, but only since there are no cars around." He winked.

Harley swung his legs over the old bike and let Alicia scoot forward to position herself comfortably. She placed her right hand firmly on the gas handle and stretched her fingers forward on her left hand to grip the clutch. Over the last few days of their vacation, Alicia had let him do most of the driving since it made her nervous being at the wheel in a foreign country, but on an open stretch of empty freeway, it seemed harmless.

"Okay, remember," Harley said patiently, now on the bike behind her and resting his chin on her left shoulder, "gas and clutch. It's just a balance between the two. Take it slow."

"Okay," she said nervously.

Alicia turned the gas grip as she slowly released the clutch, and the motorcycle inched forward onto the open road.

Harley rode behind her, yelling instructions in her ear so she could hear him.

"Good! Now grab the handles firmly when we speed up!" he shouted.

Alicia revved the accelerator, switching gears flawlessly, and the motorcycle zoomed forward. Palm trees swayed alongside the road as the couple sped blissfully along the empty highway.

"Perfect!" Harley yelled.

Alicia smiled. She relaxed her grip as she felt the warm air hit her face. She could still smell the lingering scent of the Pacific Ocean behind them. School was over, and vacation was here. Everything seemed right.

As Alicia loosened the reins on the handlebar, the old eighties motorcycle began to wobble. A loose screw fell from the skinny rusted front tire, and almost without noticing, the two-passenger bike began to drift to the left.

Harley perked up. "We're drifting!" he cautioned. "Turn it a little to the right!"

Alicia grasped tightly, but this time the handlebars were shaking in her grip, and she couldn't master them. In only a few seconds, they had drifted from one side of their lane to the other.

"I think there's something wrong!" she yelled.

"What?" Harley responded. The backseat wasn't optimal for conversing with the driver, whose voice often projected in every direction but backward.

"It's too wobbly!" she said.

Harley tried to reach around his girlfriend and take control of the motorcycle. Up ahead, about five hundred yards down the highway, he saw a large shape approaching them, too big for a car but still unidentifiable.

Franticly, he returned his eyes to the motorcycle and grabbed the leather handle grips. He tried to straighten the wavering vehicle but to no avail.

Suddenly, Alicia screamed, "Harley! Look out!"

Harley's eyes shot up again. Almost as soon as he noticed he was no longer in his own lane, he also realized what was towering toward them on their lonely two-lane highway.

As Harley's life flashed before his eyes, the last thing he remembered seeing was the bright headlights of the oncoming semitruck.

* * *

Years later, on an island in the Caribbean Sea, Jaime turned the page of a book while slouched in the cradle of a hammock. His left leg dangled from the knee to one side, and his toes brushed against the sand as he rocked back and forth. A sandy surfboard laid at his side.

Doesn't get any better than this, he thought.

It was the first week in January, and while most of his friends and family back home were bundled up inside away from the cold, Jaime was in a swimsuit and barefoot at Cabarete Beach in the Dominican Republic. Last-minute cheap flights were to blame.

"Hey, flojo," a female voice called.

"Huh?" Jaime muttered, turning over to see who was calling him.

Walking toward him with a surfboard cradled in her arms was Kennidy, one of his best friends from college. Her long baggy t-shirt draped over her one-piece swimsuit, and her dirty blonde hair dangled behind her shoulders. She looked at him with hazel eyes and nodded her head toward the ocean.

"Grab your board. Time to teach you how to use that thing." She smirked.

"Couldn't we wait just a few more minutes?" Jaime asked as he stretched his arms and yawned.

"Come on. This is what you brought me out here for. Ain't it?" she joked. "Let's go! The waves look perfect!"

A photography major during the school year, Kennidy was always down for spontaneous adventures. With flight benefits she had from her mom's employment at American Airlines, she could fly standby for free on any flight. When Jaime made the sudden decision to surf in the Dominican Republic, he knew exactly who to call.

Jaime emerged from his cozy nest in the hammock, grabbed his board, and joined Kennidy on the shoreline.

"I'm about to get worked," he said.

"Yep, no denying that. But you gotta start somewhere."

"I've only really done this a few times. What are the main things I gotta know?" he asked.

"Well, there's kind of a lot to pay attention to, so just don't give up. Surfing isn't really fun until you can stand up on a wave. Actually, it totally sucks until then, but once you can get over that hump," she said with a glimmer in her eyes, "there's nothing better."

"Fair enough," Jaime responded. "I think I'll catch on fast."

"Yeah, we'll see if you still think that after an hour."

Jaime walked slowly into the warm Caribbean Sea and dropped his board onto the surface of the water. To his left and right, the shoreline stretched out with green palm trees draping over as if to kiss the waves as they crashed onto the shore. The white sandy beach held only a few other tourists since this spot was exclusively for surfers. Jaime looked up at the rich blue sky—not a cloud in sight.

He hopped onto his board and paddled out. The waves crashed onto him until he made it past their breaking point, joining other surfers at the "lineup," the calm spot about fifty yards or so away from the shore where the surfers waited, eyeing the horizon and looking for the right wave. Kennidy was already there and began paddling just in time to catch a wave, stand up flawlessly, and ride past Jaime.

She makes that look easy, he thought.

"Nice one, Ken!" he yelled.

"Go on, amigo!" she shouted back. "Give it a go!"

Jaime sat upright on his board with his back to the shore, watching like a hawk for a perfect beginner wave—one big enough to ride, but not so big it would crush him. He bobbed in the water as smaller waves passed and other riders took their chances. He was calm and collected. He felt a laser-like focus and a total awareness of his surroundings.

I'm going to stand up on the first one.

A few yards away, he saw his chance. He kicked his feet, flipping his board around, laid his chest on the surfboard, and started paddling. With all his might, he ripped his arms through the water and tried to pick up speed. Behind him, the wave grew bigger, and Jaime could feel its tremendous force begin to push him.

I'm in the perfect spot, he said to himself.

"Good!" Kennidy yelled. "Now stand up! Quick!"

In one fluid motion, Jaime pushed up on the board with his arms and flung his legs up to a crouching position. Water splashed on his face just enough to break his focus, and without realizing his blunder, he lost his balance and leaned too far forward on his board.

He nosedived. The front of his board dug into the water, and before he knew it, the wave had flipped him upside down and hurled him into the ocean floor.

As he rose to the surface, Jaime's defeated face emerged from the white water. He heard Kennidy dying of laughter nearby.

"Woo-hoo! Nice one, man!" she teased. "I wish a had a still frame of your face before you hit the water."

Jaime paddled back into the lineup with her and sat upon his board. "Keep wishing because that's the last time that'll happen!" he countered optimistically.

"Happens to all of us. Just keep trying."

Jaime rested in the lineup for a while as he observed other surfers. He watched them as they caught a wave to learn what they were doing to make it look so easy. He noticed their form, their position on the wave, and their perfect balance on the board to avoid nose-diving.

Another surfer paddled over to him and stopped a few yards away.

"You are learning too?" he asked.

"Yeah, trying to figure it out. What about you?" Jaime asked kindly.

The man next to him was about Jaime's height, had long curly blond hair and a marked jawline. He sat upon his board and smiled, one arm swishing around in the water and the other resting awkwardly at his side at a right angle.

"Yeah, me too," he concurred. "That's my girlfriend over there catching a wave just now. I've been at this surfing thing for a few years now, but I'm still trying to get the hang of it."

"Yeah, you and me both," Jaime chuckled as he spat out a few more pieces of sand.

"Yeah, it's brutal. Most people paddle out here and just get tossed around by the waves and quit. They give up too early, but for my girlfriend and me, we're determined to get over the hump."

"Have you ever stood up before?" Jaime asked.

"Once, just once, and man, it was like nothing I'd ever done before in my life." He paused as Jaime saw him relive the moment in his eyes. "I'm not giving up 'til I do that again."

He lay back down on his board and turned back to his girlfriend. "Name's Harley, by the way, like the motorcycle. My girl over there is Alicia."

"Thanks for saying hi," Jaime said, as he too turned to paddle away. "I'm sure I'll see you around."

"Sure will!" Harley replied cheerfully.

Harley paddled away, and Jaime took another turn at catching a wave. He managed to get himself in the right position, but over and over again, he kept crashing. Lean back too much, and the board would shoot out from beneath him. Stand up too fast, and he wobbled over to one side and fell off. One time he managed to stand up but right before cheering, he realized the wave had died, and he was stationary and slowly sinking.

It seemed like every time he looked around, Kennidy was riding another wave. She made it look so easy, but Jaime, who considered himself a reasonably athletic person, was yet to stand up on a wave even once.

After several hours of trying, Jaime made his way to the shore, defeated. He sat down in the sand, placed his board to the side, and rested his arms on his bent knees, letting out an exhausted sigh.

Ocean one, Jaime zero, he thought.

In the lineup, Jaime saw Alicia and Harley trying to catch a wave. Alicia was clearly the experienced one between the two. Like Kennidy, she seemed to be the coach. With her help, Harley managed to stand up in the white water, the part of the wave most helpful for beginners. It seemed like the very act of standing up was an enormous obstacle for him.

Then Jaime saw why. As he spectated from the sand, Jaime noticed that Harley could only paddle with one arm. He also could only use his good arm to push himself up. Looking closer, Jaime saw that Harley's right arm was locked at a right angle. It was worse than useless. It was in the way.

I wonder what happened, Jaime mused.

He observed Harley a moment longer until, just in front of him, Kennidy capped a perfect ride by returning to the paddle position and coasted effortlessly back to shore. She grabbed her board, jogged over to Jaime, and plopped herself next to him.

"How'd you fair, champ?" she asked.

"You were right," Jaime admitted. "I got wrecked."

"Head up, sport," she said as she nudged his shoulder. "Keep at it. It's worth it. I promise. It's only Monday. We still got the rest of the week left."

"You make it look easy, though," Jaime said, almost bitterly.

"I've been doing this my whole life, man. You don't turn pro overnight."

"Yeah, but I've been doing this for hours, and I still couldn't stand up even once," he said pessimistically.

"Woah, woah, hang on there," Kennidy stopped him. "You're starting to sound like you're ready to throw in the towel. You're not saying you wanna quit now. Are ya?"

"No, no, obviously not," he lied. "I'm just saying I thought it would have been a bit more rewarding at first. A bit more fun. That's all."

"Psh." She laughed. "Don't expect so much at the start. You gotta work for the good stuff!"

Jaime sighed. "Yeah, maybe you're right," he relented.

"No, I definitely am," she said, half-serious. "Come on. Let's grab something to eat and get back at it."

* * *

The next few days brought some improvement, but Jaime still struggled to take the next quantum leap and ride a wave. His frustrations were growing now, and he became increasingly more impatient with each successive failure. His most recent attempt saw his ankle leash catch the soaring surfboard, ricocheting it back directly into his left rib and landing him face down in the water to fill his mouth with sand.

In the lineup again, Kennidy offered some additional coaching. "You stand up too fast. Once you push up, you gotta stay squatted until you feel totally balanced. Then you can stand."

"Yeah, but I feel like that's exactly what I'm doing," Jaime responded defensively.

"Ha-ha, it's not! You stand up like you're afraid of the water. Like there's an octopus about to bite you, and you're running away or something," she jeered.

Don't even get me started on octopus, Jaime wanted to say, as his mind flashed back to Kiribati.

"Don't be too hard on yourself, man," Jaime heard someone behind him say as Harley and Alicia made their way across the water. Harley sat upon his longboard and placed his good arm on the side to balance. "You're doing way better than we did when we first started."

"Yeah, you're way ahead of us!" Alicia agreed, sitting more comfortably on her board. Her perfectly tanned body made her blend in like a Caribbean native as she smiled cheerfully at them.

"Thanks, guys, I need the boost." Jaime sighed.

"And to keep your knees bent!" Kennidy added.

"Well, whenever you're done practicing, why don't you come on over and join us for lunch?" Alicia invited.

"Sounds great to me," Jaime said. "I could go for another Dominican bowl for a refuel."

"We'll be there!" Kennidy chimed in.

"Sweet!" Harley said. "Good luck!"

They both paddled away, and Kennidy leaned over to Jaime and spoke softly.

"Did you see them too?" she whispered.

"See what?" Jaime asked.

"The scars," she said.

"Scars?"

"Yeah, all over, on both of them," she said. "I think that's why Harley's armed is locked like that."

"That would make sense," Jaime admitted. "Well, if you're thinking about asking them about it, it might be a sensitive subject."

"Nah, I'm sure they get it all the time," Kennidy said. "Plus, I bet there's a cool story behind it. Don't you think?"

"Eh... maybe."

* * *

A stone's throw away from the shore was the only restaurant on the beach, El Dominicano—famous for their Dominican bowls with rice, beans, plantains, guacamole, and a fried egg. Jaime and Kennidy grabbed their order from the counter and turned to find a place to sit. Jaime ducked his head as he stepped into the canopy dining area composed of five tables on the sand and looked around for their lunch appointment. Already seated, Alicia and Harley motioned to them by waving their hands.

"Looks good," Alicia said. "What did you get?"

"Dominican bowls, both of us," Jaime said excitedly.

"Same with us. We've gotten it every day this week." She laughed.

Harley brushed one hand through his long hair and then rested his arms on the table. "How'd you guys do today?" he asked.

"Awesome!" Kennidy said. "The waves were so nice."

"Ha, maybe for you!" Jaime joked. "Still no breakthroughs for me. I'm still getting pummeled out there."

"Ah, don't worry about it," Harley tried to cheer him up. "It's all about getting more time in the water."

Jaime nodded in agreement as he took a gargantuan bite out of his food.

"How long have you been surfing?" Kennidy asked.

"We started together on a trip in Costa Rica about four years ago," Alicia answered. "It's been on and off since then since we had to take a break and can only surf on vacation."

"What about you guys?" Harley asked.

"I've been surfing my whole life in California," Kennidy answered, "but Jaime's career started just a few days ago."

"And it might end in a few days too," he muttered.

"Ah, come off it," Kennidy joked.

"Nah, you're doing great, man. You look much better than me out there with this gimp limb of mine," Harley said as he jokingly swayed his arm.

Kennidy took advantage of the mention. "Yeah, we noticed that," she said, as she felt Jaime nudge her knee under the table, "and a lot of the cool scars you guys both have. We were wondering if there was some cool story behind all of it!"

"But you definitely don't have to tell us if it's uncomfortable," Jaime blurted out, trying to be polite.

"No, not at all. People ask all the time, and we're used to talking about it," Alicia said.

Jaime felt a sharp nudge back. "Told you," he thought he heard Kennidy say.

"It actually happened in Costa Rica when we started surfing," Harley began. "We had rented a motorcycle for the two weeks we were on vacation, and I was helping Alicia learn how to ride the first few days. Everything was going well, and we didn't think anything bad was going to happen."

"On our last day," Alicia continued, "we had just left the beach and were driving down the highway when I asked Harley if I could drive. Something happened, and we lost control and, well, we drifted into the oncoming lane and got hit head-on by a semitruck."

Kennidy gasped, and Jaime's jaw dropped.

"We both flew from the bike," Harley said. "I landed about twenty yards away from Alicia. I knew immediately I had broken both of my legs and my arm. I tried calling to Alicia, but she was unconscious and out of reach. Nobody was around, so I tried using my only good arm to crawl toward her, but I couldn't get far before the pain was too much. Luckily, a passing car pulled over and called an ambulance. We were rushed to the hospital."

"Oh my gosh," Jaime whispered.

"You should have died!" Kennidy gasped.

"It was honestly a miracle," Harley agreed. "We were in bad shape for a while. It took several months for bones to recover and burns to heal, but we survived. Alicia was actually in a coma for the first month of it."

"You're kidding me," Jaime said, dumbfounded.

"Yeah, I woke up with my parents in the hospital with me and not able to move. Luckily, I didn't have any permanent damage except for these scars," she said as she ran her fingers up her chest, revealing a purple mark where doctors had operated in addition to the marks on her cheek, forehead, hip, and both arms.

"I wasn't as lucky," Harley said. "The doctors did all they could, and they did a great job, but unfortunately, the best they could do for this arm was to leave it like this, locked up and permanently stuck in this position," he looked down and flexed his arm in and out, showing how his arm was completely locked at the elbow, preventing any straightening.

"Oh my gosh," Kennidy whispered. "I'm so sorry. That must have been so traumatic."

"Yeah, it was pretty rough," Alicia said. "But again, we are just lucky to be alive. Life after the accident has been a gift, and we are grateful for every day."

"Yeah," Jaime said, "I believe that." He paused as he examined Harley's scar-covered arm. He thought about how hard it must be for Harley to try to push himself up on a surfboard.

"So," Jaime began, "it's been several years now, and here you are back on the surfboard with only one arm. Why?"

Harley smiled. "Man, people these days are starting things and leaving them a second later. We are all about instant gratification, and if something ever gets hard, we just quit. We expect a life given to us on a silver platter. I don't want that mentality to get to me.

"When I got to Costa Rica, I wanted to learn how to surf, and I ain't gonna let this accident stop me from getting there, even if I have to do it with only one arm. I'm gonna see it through 'til I can stand up routinely."

"Wait," Kennidy said, "You're telling me that four years after your accident, and you're still committed to catching a wave?"

Harley laughed and almost instinctively recited words that seemed like second nature to him:

"When a task is once begun, leave it not until it's done. Whether the matter be big or small, do it well, or not at all.

"My dad taught me those words as I kid," he said. "I've always remembered them. He taught me how to have grit, how to persevere when times are tough, no matter the task. Sure, it's only surfing, but the principle still applies. I want to prove to myself that I can triumph no matter what's in my way."

Jaime was silent.

He was mostly embarrassed that he had considered quitting surfing after only a few days while Harley had endured through years of struggle without a single thought of giving up.

"I've got a lot to learn from you," Jaime said. "You truly are incredible. I can only imagine what you are doing with the rest of your life."

"How you do one thing is how you do everything." Harley laughed. "I don't know. I'm either extremely stubborn or just downright determined."

"Well, whichever it is, I could use a pinch of it." Jaime laughed.

* * *

On their last day, Jaime said goodbye to his new friends before leaving the beach. He didn't catch a wave, but it no longer mattered. *Time in the water,* he thought. *I'll get there eventually.*

When he said goodbye, Harley wrapped his gimp arm around Jaime in a hug and patted his back.

"Life can hit hard, much harder than these waves were hitting you," he said bluntly, setting his good arm on Jaime's shoulder and looking him in the eye. "Trust me, I know. It hit me with a truck."

Jaime let out a chuckle. "True."

"But no matter the obstacle," he continued, "you never give up."

"Right," Jaime said. "Thank you. I'll remember that."

"You'll get over the hump soon enough. I'm sure of it," Harley said reassuringly, as he grabbed his board with his good arm and headed back out.

Jaime packed his things and walked toward the parking lot. Kennidy was waiting for him in a Taxi that would be taking them back to the airport. In a few hours, he would be back in the states enduring the grueling cold of winter. Jaime embraced the last sensation of the sand between his toes and the Caribbean air blowing against his face.

He gave a final glance back at the ocean as if to say goodbye. Just then, for a moment, he saw Harley leaving the lineup, standing up on his board and riding a wave with one triumphant arm raised in the air.

* * *

Jaime put his hands in his pockets as he walked from one side of the stage to the other before addressing the audience. It was routine now. He felt comfortable on stage after four weeks of lecturing. As he looked at his audience, he noted an increase in numbers again. Not only had more people attended this session, but by some miracle, there seemed to be almost no multitasking. All phones, laptops, and other distractions were stored away, and everyone was paying attention.

"I wish I had learned this lesson myself when I was in your shoes," Jaime began. "I wonder how many opportunities I gave up on too early.

"As Harley said, we all live in an age of instant gratification. I was the perfect example of that when I was learning to surf. I wanted to get the benefits of the sport without putting in the work. Similarly, our generation has everything we could ever want at the tip of our fingertips, and we are hesitant to pursue anything outside of that reach. We quit things too early without actually giving them a try, and that leaves us feeling lost, incompetent, empty, and without purpose in the world.

"Surfing wasn't Harley's vocation in life, but we can learn something from his dedication to even the smallest of things.

Imagine how much you and I could change our lives if we had the kind of grit in our pursuits that Harley showed in his life."

The audience was quiet as Jaime neared the end of his lecture. Per routine, he left a few moments for questions from the crowd.

"Mr. Gonzalez," said a student, raising a hand. "One of the blessings of technology today is the very ability to try all kinds of new things. Because we have so much at our fingertips, we can give it all a try! I think for me, the difficulty lies in knowing what things I need to quit, and what things are worth enduring."

"You bring up a great point, but I think the answer is actually simpler than you think," Jaime responded. "The only way to truly know if something is worth enduring is to endure it for a moment! If you want to know if a new workout routine is actually functioning, it would be foolish to meticulously check for results every day in the mirror. Only by allotting a reasonable amount of time to monitor results could you determine if your efforts were worth the reward. So, if you are still wondering if something is worth enduring, you probably haven't endured long enough."

As he finished his answer, a few students stood to leave, and Jaime realized he was almost out of time.

"Thank you all for joining me this week," he said as the clock ticked past the final minute and more students began to stand and vacate the auditorium. "There are only two more weeks left in these lecture series, so as Harley would say, don't quit yet! I have a few more important lessons I'd like to discuss before we part ways."

The lights turned on followed by the sound of shuffling feet as the audience returned to the world outside the auditorium doors.

CHAPTER 6

THE SCHOOL

Jaime stared out the window of the volunteer bus as it drove away from the rundown elementary school. It was his last day of work, and it was raining.

"Hey, man, you okay?" his friend Mack asked.

Jaime kept his eyes on the school with his forehead pressed to the glass and didn't respond.

Mack brushed off the rejection and patted his friend on the shoulder. "It's okay, man. Let me know if you need anything."

Jaime paid him little attention. He wasn't being rude; he just wanted to be alone.

He looked back at the school and saw the horde of kids outside. He thought of Ayelen, of her future, and of the future of all the kids there.

The old bus drove on, running over divots, splashing mud on the curb, and honking at cars as it continued on its way to the hostel where Jaime would pack his things and return home to his life in the US.

It's not fair, he thought.

As the school faded from view, he cried.

* * *

The smell of fried eggs and rice still lingered in the air as several travelers made their way from breakfast to the meeting room. A short woman strutted to the front and cleared her throat.

"Welcome, everyone, to our new volunteer orientation," the lady said. She was a local to Asunción, yet her English was flawless. She had given this same introduction many times to previous groups of volunteers.

"Thank you all for coming to Paraguay and for joining us in this construction project. We are so grateful for your help."

Seated on the sofa in an oval-shaped room, Jaime leaned back and crossed his legs at the ankles. He looked around and saw seven or so volunteers who had come from around the world. They were all signed up to participate in the construction of a new classroom for a school district nearby.

Jaime rolled up the sleeves of his favorite blue jean button-up and listened as the speaker continued.

"As you might already know, La Jacinta neighborhood is a very poor area, and this new classroom will be so important to the students there. You will help provide them with the environment and education that could change their lives. We cannot thank you enough. Muchas gracias," she said, as she clasped her hands and bowed her head to the group.

Jaime joined with others in applause. He remained seated on the comfy couch as the meeting adjourned and his fellow volunteers wandered back to their rooms. He stretched his arms, leaned his head back, and released a mighty yawn. His flight had landed the night before and was once again an itinerary of red-eyes and long layovers, the sufferings of a travel-hungry college student.

"Didn't sleep much?" asked a stocky man passing by.

Jaime chuckled. "The airport chairs in Bogotá didn't make for the best bed," he joked.

"No kidding. I flew through Guatemala. Didn't get more than an hour of shuteye." The man yawned as well as he rubbed his eyes and sat down beside Jaime.

"I'm Mack," he said, extending a hand.

"Jaime. Nice to meet you," Jaime responded, shaking his hand.

"How'd you find out about this gig?" Mack asked.

Jaime shrugged. "I've always loved to travel. I'm in school right now, but I always try and sneak in a trip or two between semesters. I've met some really cool people and seen the world, but I felt like I could do something different this time.

I wanted not to just visit people from a different country but do something for them."

"That's really cool," Mack responded softly. He had a thick beard that covered most of his face. He spoke in a deep, soothing voice as if he were the baritone in his church choir.

"What about you?" Jaime asked.

"My dad was in the Peace Corps down here for a few years and always talked it up. I figured I had to come down here myself and see what was so great about it, and if I'm down here, I might as well do something helpful while I'm at it. Plus, I want to practice my Spanish."

"That's cool," Jaime said. "Ever done any construction before? I hope they don't have us working any power tools."

"Ha-ha, don't worry. I think we will be laying a lot of bricks and making cement, things like that. It will be pretty basic. You don't need previous experience. Plus, nobody could afford any power tools down here even if they wanted them."

"Well, I'm excited to get started."

"Me too," Mack said as he pressed his hands on his knees and stood up. "Well, I'm going to go catch some Z's, but I'll see you tomorrow at the workplace."

"Yeah, I should head to bed too," Jaime agreed.

"See you in the morning," Mack said as he left.

Lying in his bed, Jaime rested his head against the wall and gazed at the ceiling. Sleep was winning him over, but he kept thinking about their future construction project. How many kids would be using the school? How many mothers would drop them off at the entrance each day for class? He smiled, imagining the impact the school would bring to the poor community.

This could make all the difference for them, he thought. *We are going to change their future.*

As volunteers chatted in the distance, Jaime's eyes slowly dropped, and he drifted off into a much-needed sleep, sure that his service would be impactful.

* * *

The next morning, Jaime rose with the half-dozen or so volunteers and boarded a local school bus that carried them to the new worksite fifteen minutes away.

La Jacinta neighborhood.

They drove by muddy rivers, passed mountains of bundled up trash, and bumped over numerous potholes scattered in the streets. The neighborhood's rundown infrastructure and poorly kept public roads extended the trip, despite the worksite being a short distance away.

The bus came to a stop, and Jaime stepped onto the unpaved road and looked across the street at his project site. Secundaria La Jacinta. A paint-scraped archway stood at the entrance.

Hanging from the middle was a welcome sign in a bright red hue that read "Bienvenido, Alumnos!" Welcome, Students!

Passing through the archway, Jaime came face to face with the school grounds. On his left was the courtyard, roughly the size of a normal basketball court. Two soccer goals without nets marked the beginning and end of the open space, and next to it was the school itself. The small structure occupied about the same space as the courtyard but crammed in three different classrooms. He could hear the sounds of children at their desks, some yelling and screaming. It didn't sound like very much learning was taking place.

"This way, amigos!" a pudgy man called to Jaime and the group. "Worksite is over here!"

As Jaime headed over, he saw Mack trudge up next to him.

"Morning, amigo," he said.

"Buenos días." Jaime smiled back.

"You ready to get to work?"

"Could hardly fall asleep last night just thinking about it!" Jaime joked as he yawned, still tired from his previous flight.

"Me too. I think the worksite is just on the property right next to us."

The pudgy man led them around the school building and revealed the vacant property next to it. The open space was about the same size as the school, and construction seemed to be just beginning.

The pudgy man then stepped to the front of them. He was about Jaime's height, five foot eight inches or so, but about fifty pounds heavier. He had a large belly covered by his checkered and worn button-up, and his blue jeans had rips and tears in them from years on the job.

"This will be where we build the school!" he said in accented English. "My crew and I have already laid the foundation. We need your help laying the bricks and making cement."

Jaime leaned over to Mack. "You were spot on," he whispered.

"I'm Pablo, and I'll be the chief foreman here. This is my team behind you—Carlos, Alex, and Matías. They will help you stay organized."

Jaime swung his head around and saw the three young men, early twenties or so, nod.

"Bien," he said. "Let's get you into groups."

Pablo divided up the volunteers into groups of two or three with the assistants. Mack and Jaime stuck together as Matías made his way over to them.

"Hola," he said. "Nice to meet you. I'm Matías."

"Nice to meet you, Matías," Jaime and Mack said in unison.

"Let's work together, the three of us. Está bien?"

"Perfecto," Jaime answered back, trying to speak in the best Spanish accent he could.

Matías was a skinnier worker and the foreman's son. He wore a construction hat that was too big for his head and carried with him a clipboard and a pencil between his ear to give off the impression that he was some kind of administrator. Despite the show, he was incredibly fun to be around and got on well with Jaime and Mack.

"This is where we will begin," Matías said. "I brought you everything you need: gloves, trowel, and buckets." He pointed over to an orange machine placed in the center of the worksite. "That is our cement maker. We will have to put cement into the buckets and bring it over here to use for laying bricks. The bricks are outside, and we will also have to grab those and bring them to our spot."

"And how exactly do you lay a brick?" Jaime asked.

"It's easy," Matías said as if it were nothing. "Here, I show you."

"Matías grabbed a single brick from the stack he had brought over earlier and knelt down next to the fence that bordered the worksite. He scooped the trowel into the bucket of cement and plopped it down on the ground in a perfectly rectangular blob.

"Place the cement like this," he said. "Not too much, not too little. Then, lay the brick on top and fit it nicely into the cement. Once you do that, do it again right next to the brick you just laid, like this." He laid another brick.

"You have to make sure they are level," he added, as he dropped down on the ground and eyed the tops of each brick, ensuring that they were even with each other. "Uneven foundation will lead to an unstable house," he said with a smile.

Mack cracked a subtle grin.

"And that's it! Let's get to it!"

Jaime and Mack looked at each other and chuckled.

"Alrighty then," Mack said, "Looks easy enough. Come on, Jaime."

The pair put their gloves on and stocked their location with plenty of bricks and cement to last them the next few hours. They lay brick after brick along the fence, covering a distance of almost thirty yards or so. They both worked tirelessly with the utmost precision, ensuring the bricks were even and stable.

After finishing a single row of thirty bricks or so, Jaime checked his watch. It was nearly noon. They had worked for almost three hours and only finished a single row.

"We are going so slowly," Jaime breathed. "There's got to be some kind of secret to this,"

Mack nodded in agreement. He looked over his shoulder and gasped. "You're kidding me," he said.

"What?" Jaime asked.

"Look at how far Matías is."

Jaime turned to see Matías working on another corner and noticed he had finished three rows of bricks. It looked a lot prettier than theirs.

"How did he do that so fast?" Mack asked.

"Let's find out. Oi, Matías!" he yelled. "How'd you do that?"

"Qué?" Matías paused as he looked in their direction and walked over to listen closely.

"What's the secret to this thing?" Jaime asked, puzzled.

"Secret?" Matías asked, seemingly confused himself.

"Yeah, you know, the shortcut. How can we get moving as fast as you?"

Matías chuckled. "Hard work, amigo! I've done this for a long time. Just do your best. You'll get it."

Jaime shook his head.

"Did he say hard work?" Mack asked.

"Yeah. Some shortcut." He sighed.

Jaime and Mack shook their heads and continued working. It seemed that no matter how hard they worked, they couldn't seem to keep pace with Matías.

During breaks, they often ate lunch in the center courtyard where the school children had recess and watched them play soccer. Jaime watched as young elementary school futbolistas would handle the soccer ball like it was second nature. Boys and girls of all ages would play without any discrimination.

Occasionally, Jaime and Mack joined in.

One of the children, in particular, caught Jaime's eye. Her name was Ayelen, a third-grader with a smile that made time stop. Ayelen was a social bug, full of energy and life, jumping from one friend circle to another. In one moment, she was with the girls her age playing with blocks and dolls in the classroom, and the next, she was playing soccer with the fifth years pushing and shoving as if she were one of them. Yet despite her assertive moments, Ayelen was the most tender child Jaime had ever met.

One day, he joined her at the table in a classroom and asked her name.

"Ayelen," she responded.

"That's a beautiful name," Jaime said.

Ayelen smiled and blushed.

"Do you speak English?" Jaime asked.

Ayelen laughed. "One, two, three!" she yelled with a smirk. Her friends chuckled behind her.

"Ha-ha, you can count! Not bad." Jaime smiled.

Jaime didn't know much about this little girl, but something about her captivated him. Maybe it was her connection to many different friend circles, but for some reason she felt like Jaime's connection to the school.

"Are you excited about your new classroom, Ayelen?" Jaime asked. She continued drawing, blushing to herself, either too shy to answer or unsure what he said.

"We're building you a classroom, Ayelen, so you can become really smart," Jaime said. He hoped the essence of his words would somehow sink in.

"I hope you like it," he added.

As Jaime stood to leave, he felt a tug at his leg. He looked down to see Ayelen wrapping her arms around him.

"Gracias!" she squealed and then ran off with her friends giggling.

Jaime watched them leave the room as Ayelen's dusty hair bounced in her ponytail and disappeared from view.

From behind him, a friendly voice spoke to him in almost perfect English. "Thank you for what you are doing."

Jaime turned to see a teacher from the school smiling.

"What you are doing for these children, you have no idea what it means to us," she said.

"Oh, of course. It's nothing really, just here to help," Jaime muttered.

"These kids," she said, as she moved toward the window with her arms crossed, watching the kids at recess, "come from tough backgrounds. Most of them will not graduate high school. Many of the girls will become pregnant before eighteen. Their future is very dim."

"That's… that's terrible," Jaime said.

"We teach them the best we can, but multiple factors are at play here. We never know how much we can really do."

Jaime looked at her as she spoke. She seemed to gaze at the kids with some sort of helpless desperation. Her wrinkly skin showed years of experience and empathy, and Jaime wished he could do more.

"Sometimes we feel like we are the only ones helping these young kids, so when we see kind people like you come to help, it reinvigorates our spirits."

"Well, thank you," Jaime said. "I'm glad we are helping." He paused a moment to think about what she had just said.

"But you mean most of them don't even continue in school?" Jaime asked.

"Sadly, yes, that's the reality," she said somberly. "Crime, drugs, theft. Too many temptations pick them out one by one. It's the sad truth."

"What happens to them after they drop out?"

"They fall into the same cycle. They stay poor, their kids stay poor and come to poor schools like ours, and they repeat the cycle."

"How do they get out?"

"Several of them find their way, stay in school, and manage to make it through college and get a good job, but those cases are definitely the minority."

Something uncomfortable stirred inside Jaime. His previous perspective of coming to Paraguay to serve the children and change the world suddenly seemed like a childish and silly dream. *There's no hope here,* he thought. *What's the point?*

He felt sick.

"I should get back to work," he said.

The teacher nodded, and Jaime returned to the worksite to finish his tasks before getting on the bus and heading back to the hostel. Moments before pulling away, he caught a glimpse of Ayelen's mother coming to pick up her daughter from school. She was young, no older than her early twenties, and looked as if she could have been a student only a few years earlier. Ayelen embraced her with an endearing hug, and the two left together holding hands, returning to their life in La Jacinta neighborhood.

Pretending it wasn't real, he lifted himself onto the bus and sat down in the back by himself.

"Hey, man, you okay?" Mack asked as the bus rolled on back to the hostel.

Jaime didn't want to talk. The bus rolled over more divots, and Jaime shifted in his chair, but his gaze remained fixed outside the window.

As he kept to his corner and looked out at the dirt roads and cement houses, tears began to roll down his cheeks. As much as he wished he could forget everything the schoolteacher had just told him, he knew it was useless. He had never felt more depressed. It was as if every effort he exerted into this experience was a total waste.

He didn't say a word the entire ride home.

* * *

Back at the hostel, Jaime, Mack, and another volunteer named Jason shot the breeze over a game of cards.

"It's your turn," Jason said to Mack. Jason was a Michigan Grad taking a celebratory tour through South America as a graduation gift to himself. He stuffed popcorn down his throat as he vigilantly monitored the pace of the game.

Mack laid down a card and took a glimpse at Jaime. His hair was messy, and his eyes were still a bit swollen from his silent ride home on the bus earlier.

"I saw you were talking to the teacher today," he said, as Jaime raised his head.

"Yeah," Jaime breathed. His shoulders slumped, and he sank into his chair.

"You've been quiet most of the night," Mack added.

"Yeah."

"Did she say something?"

"Your turn, Mack," Jason butted in with a brisk tone.

Jaime continued, "I don't know. Just some things about the kids and stuff."

"Like what stuff?" Mack said.

"Just that the kids don't have great odds. So much is out of their control and affects their future, and they can't do anything about it. It's just a little depressing to think about."

"Yeah," Mack said quietly. "Yeah, that is a little depressing." He looked at the ground, trying to find comforting words to say, but none came.

"Yeah, I mean, all the work we're putting in. What is it all worth? What's the point?" Jaime's voice was escalating. Jason and Mack could feel the mood in the room suddenly change.

"Yeah, and it's only making it worse that it's still your turn again, and we are all waiting on you," Jason said, stuffing another handful of popcorn into his mouth.

Jaime leaned forward in his chair and tried to feign interest in the game, but he could feel his blood rise.

"It just makes me feel like it's not even worth it," Jaime said. "All this effort."

"How do you mean?" Jason asked, joining the conversation.

"You're talking about the school?" Mack asked.

"No, not just this school. Everything. I know I'm not in the same situation as here, but it's the same thing if you think about it. No matter how hard any of us work in life, so many different things can happen to us that we have no control over whatsoever. Losing a job, getting sick, losing family or friends." Jaime was almost quiet now, his madness transforming into hopelessness. "I guess it kind of just makes me want to give up."

Mack had no response. There was a long moment of silence as they stared at the table aimlessly. Neither tried to calm him down. They knew it was useless.

The silence was broken by the sound of popcorn being inhaled by a ravenous creature.

"Mack, it's your turn," Jason croaked.

* * *

Jaime's sullen mood persisted over the next few days at the worksite. He worked slowly. His legs felt heavy, his arms felt like weights, and he lacked any motivation to continue working as he had before.

Noticing his dampened spirit, Matías made his way over from his station and attempted to cheer up his partner.

"Qué pasó, amigo?" he asked. "You seem off. What happened to working hard?"

"I'm just not feeling it today."

"Well, looks like someone over there wants to see you," Matías said, pointing off toward the school.

Jaime lifted his eyes and saw the school children at recess. Leaning against one of the pillars that supported the school's welcome sign, the same teacher Jaime had spoken to a few days earlier was waiting for him.

"I'm afraid I left you in a bit of a depressing state the other day," she said embarrassingly.

"Sort of," Jaime admitted.

"Well, I'm sorry about that. But I shouldn't have left you without giving you a piece of hope to hold on to. It's why I still come to work every day and why I continue doing what I do. It's the only thing you can do too when you're back home facing your own challenges and stresses that life will inevitably bring."

"What is it?" Jaime asked inquisitively.

"There is only one thing we can do in life, *mijo*," she said. "We can do our best."

She stood up from her leaning position, placed her arms on Jaime's shoulders, and gazed into his soul.

"The only thing one ever can do is give their best effort. In life, so many factors are out of our control. We simply need not focus on these things. At any given moment, the only thing that is one hundred percent within our control is our own effort. That is why I keep teaching. That is why I work hard. Because it's the only thing I can do."

"But, what's the point," Jaime asked, "if it might all be pointless?"

"That is not for me to decide. If I don't do my part, it will certainly, most positively be in vain! Yet, somehow, I've learned over the years that everything not within our control pales in comparison to all that is. If we simply do our best, we will give ourselves the best chances for success. Those who give up and surrender to life's circumstances rob themselves of a chance for a better future. I won't do that, and I hope Ayelen doesn't either. I hope she beats the odds as well as the rest of my students. I hope they do their best, but again, that is not for me to decide. All I can focus on is my own effort."

Jaime paused, attempting to reconcile her words with the dim reality he struggled with a few nights before. His thoughts raced back to Matías a few days prior, when Jaime asked him what the shortcut was to laying bricks. "Hard work," he had said. "Do your best."

The teacher lowered her arms from Jaime's shoulder, took his hands in hers, and kissed them. Then she whispered softly to him.

"There is always hope where there is effort."

She let go of his hands and then retired to her corner of the school. Jaime stood there alone and stared at the ground for a moment, pondering the teacher's words.

Across the courtyard, Ayelen played at recess with her friends. Her innocent laugh echoed off the walls. Jaime caught her eye for a moment and motioned her to come over. She left her friends and skipped across the school, stopping at Jaime's feet.

"Here," Jaime said, kneeling down to her level. "I want you to have this."

With his right hand, Jaime removed the bracelet Prosper had given him on the summit of Mount Kilimanjaro and tied it to Ayelen's little wrist.

"Para mi?" she said.

"Yes, for you." He smiled. "Hold on to this, okay? It's been with me through a lot, and I want you to have it." He knew she probably didn't understand him, but he said it anyway.

She blushed. "Gracias!" she said as she gave him a final hug.

Jaime watched as she scurried back to her friends. He rose back to his feet, turned around, and headed back to finish his last day at La Jacinta.

* * *

Jaime brought himself to center stage once more and added a few finishing touches to his story.

"My nonconformist approach to life taught me a valuable lesson in Paraguay. I learned to focus only on what is within my control, and then to execute with one hundred percent effort.

"Many people nowadays are constantly looking for a shortcut in life, some secret that will launch them to success without ever getting their feet dirty in the trenches. Others either get distracted by tasks that seem overbearing or by other people who make them feel small. I've learned that the only solution to these problems is to do your best. Anything less, and you will return home at the end of the day, look yourself in the mirror, and know you have cheated yourself and the world of a better future. That, my friends, will be the biggest letdown of our lives.

"If, however, we commit to doing our best, we guarantee pride and satisfaction in the results. John Wooden, the famed UCLA basketball coach, was a man who championed this very idea. It has led him and the Bruins to ten national championships in twelve years. He once said,

"Success comes from knowing that you did your best to become the best that you are capable of becoming. Things turn out best for the people who make the best of the way things turn out. Do not let what you cannot do interfere with what you can do. Just do the best you can. No one can do more than that."[8]

From the back of the room, a hand emerged. Jaime nodded his head, and the young student spoke.

"Don't you think it's ignorant to ignore all other factors except for your own effort?" the boy asked.

"I'm not saying to ignore them," Jaime began. "It's always important to be aware, but being aware and worrying about those factors are two totally different things. It is wasted energy to worry about something that is completely out of your control. It is not, however, wasted energy if that worry ignites action, because now you can work hard on something. But if the end result leads you to a dead-end of worry, you've done nothing but hurt yourself."

As he finished, he saw another student in the middle section raise her hand.

---

8   John Wooden, "Motivational Quotes," The Wooden Effect, accessed November 23, 2020.

"Some people would say that comparison spurs progress. You don't always know what your best is, and when you have someone to compare yourself to, that might inspire you to work harder. What would you say to that?" she said.

"That makes sense," Jaime agreed, "but it is a dangerous downhill slope. Going along with the world of athletics, see what legendary Penn State football coach Joe Paterno had to say about that topic:

"'There are many people, particularly in sports, who think that success and excellence are the same thing. They are not the same things. Excellence is something that is lasting and dependable and largely within a person's control. In contrast, success is perishable and is often outside our control. If you strive for excellence, you will probably be successful eventually. People who put excellence in the first place have the patience to end up with success. An additional burden for the victim of the success mentality is that he is threatened by the success of others, and he resents real excellence. In contrast, the person that is fascinated by quality is excited when he sees it in others.'[9]

"So, sure," he summarized, "comparison might push you to work hard, but in the end, it may be a cancer to you that will constantly leave you feeling like you are not good enough."

Jaime paused before wrapping up, waiting for any last-minute questions to emerge. Seeing a silent audience, he checked the clock.

Another week had come to a close.

---

9   "Joe Paterno Quotes," Goodreads, accessed November 23, 2020

CHAPTER 7

THE LAST LECTURE

The sky was clear as Jaime strutted along his normal path to the University of Washington on his last day of the lecture series.

He arrived early only to find the auditorium half full. Students had their laptops open and worked on other classwork while awaiting the final lecture.

Jaime took advantage of the time to greet some of the students. He walked through the aisle and shook their hands.

"It's been incredible," one said. "Really awesome, sir!" piped another.

Jaime blushed at the compliments. He thanked each one for coming and listened to a few tell their stories of how they, too, felt pressured to fit a mold.

The clock above the door struck the hour, and Jaime drifted to center stage and welcomed his audience for the last time.

"Good morning!" he said cheerfully. "I'm honored, and a bit sad, I admit, to be addressing you this morning. Today is the last lecture of this series, and it has been an incredible time with all of you."

Brief applause cut him off before he could continue.

"Today, our time will be brief. I wish only to summarize all that we have learned during this lecture series and add a few disclaimers."

The auditorium, full now with every seat taken and a few students standing along the walls, was silent as listeners scooted to the edge of their seats to hear their speaker's final words.

"When I made the decision years ago not to conform," Jaime started reminiscently, "my life was presented with a world of opportunities and lessons that were tailor-made for me. The purpose of my lectures was to urge you to do the same. When you take a nonconformist, individualistic approach to life, you will experience a wonderful world of discoveries."

The room was dark now. The lights dimmed and the bright summer's day outside was blocked by the window blinds. A single light shone on Jaime, and he could only make out the faint outline of faces staring at the stage.

"I figured for today, we would review all we have learned thus far."

Jaime clicked a button on the remote control in his hand, and an image appeared on the giant projector screen behind him.

Students quickly recognized it as a dimly lit path leading to the top of Africa's highest peak.

"On Mount Kilimanjaro, we learned how to act amidst uncertainty. When the future is dark before us, the only way to proceed is by putting one foot in front of the other and going step by step."

Click. Another mountain, covered in snow, appeared before them.

"On Everest, we learned the importance of humility and that there is plenty of room at the top. As we recognize our smallness in the world, it prompts us to look to our left and right and lend a hand to those around us."

Click. A stick hut perched along the shores of the Pacific.

"In the islands of Kiribati, we immersed ourselves in a new culture that forced us to reevaluate how we treat others. Regardless of race, ethnicity, culture, or nationality, we must choose to show love. This has been the single greatest truth taught by all major religions of the world, and we would do well to follow its council."

Click. Surfers holding their boards, walking out to a beautiful blue ocean.

"In the Dominican Republic, we learned from our dear friends Harley and Alicia the importance of grit. No matter how hard life hits—even when it's a semitruck—we can choose not to make excuses and, instead, persevere. Hold on, and push through when times are hard. Anything worth doing will always have its bumps. As the American publisher William Feather once said, 'Success seems to be largely a matter of hanging on after others have let go.'"

Jaime clicked again, and the screen went black. He emerged from the side of the stage with his arms folded, and his hand gently stroking his chin.

A flash of light and a group of young students smiled underneath a welcome sign of an elementary school.

"In Paraguay, we learned the invaluable lesson that the only shortcut in life is hard work. We will never be able to control every aspect of our life, but we can choose to focus on those things we can control. As we do this, we do the only thing in our power to set us up for success. Destiny often takes care of itself after that.

"Now, I have given a lecture on the benefits of nonconformity," Jaime said, "but I feel I need to reiterate a few things." He looked toward the ceiling pensively, as if carefully forming his next few words.

"Nonconformity is not rebellion. As I mentioned at the beginning of our meetings, I am not calling for a revolt against mainstream behavior. I am simply inviting you to consider doing things differently. A true nonconformist approach to life is about finding our own individuality and becoming something, not rebelling against something.

"Another point I would like to clarify is along a similar vein. Nonconformity is not simply about being different. While being distinct from the traditional course, nonconformists are not simply on a mission to be different from the rest. They are simply on a mission to be true to themselves. If this happens to be different from the norm, they are okay with that."

Jaime clicked a button again, and a quote appeared on the wall behind him.

"Martin Luther King once said,

"'There is a type of bad nonconformity. There is no virtue in being a nonconformist just to be a nonconformist. Some people are nonconformist just to get attention and to be different.'

"If we are so focused on the crowd and determined to be different from them, we are essentially being controlled by external circumstances and are conforming to outside pressures. This, my friends, is the exact opposite of what we are trying to accomplish."

He clicked his controller again, and the words behind him vanished, leaving an empty screen. The stage light focused in on Jaime as he brought himself to the front, only a few feet away from the students in the first row.

"My final caution on nonconformity is that it is not meant to be a selfish outlook. While being a nonconformist implies finding our own individuality, the word 'individual' should not be understood to mean selfish. We seek our own individuality to be true to ourselves, but with the aim to add value to the world. We do not make life decisions without thinking of how our actions impact other people, nor are we seeking to distance ourselves from those who are different from us. A nonconformist refuses to conform to a crowd, but they do not refuse to interact with them."

Jaime stared out into the audience and saw blackness. He could only see a faint outline of the faces that had watched him over the previous weeks.

"With that, my friends, our time has come to a close." He paused a moment and looked at his audience. He thought of the final words he would leave the group with, but only a few came to mind.

"As you take a nonconformist approach to life, I think you will soon realize that if your life path seems to drift off course from the norm, that might be a good thing."

As Jaime finished speaking, there was a brief moment of silence, and time seemed to stand still. For a moment, Jaime felt as if he were alone on the stage in an empty auditorium.

Bringing him back to reality was a roar of applause and the audience rising to their feet.

* * *

Jaime stood by the door and shook hands with students as they exited. A line built up, extending far up the stairs of the auditorium, and Jaime felt as if his hand would fall off.

When the last person finally approached him, Jaime thought he recognized her. A purple sweater with an inscription on it identified her as a member of the university's student body presidency. She hugged her books against her chest with both arms as she drew closer.

"I just want to say thank you," the girl said as she presented herself in front of Jaime. She was very tan-skinned with her hair in a beautiful ponytail. "You really changed my life."

Jaime blushed. "Well, thank you so much," he answered, "but I don't know if I can take that much credit. It was only a lecture series, after all."

"No, I wasn't talking about that," she answered. She extended her arm out to shake Jaime's hand, and the sleeve of her sweater rolled up just slightly enough so that a familiar bracelet Jaime had gifted to a young Paraguayan girl many years before became visible.

Jaime looked back at the girl he now recognized.

"Ayelen," he whispered as he shook her hand.

"Thank you for helping me start my own journey," she said softly. She withdrew her hand, pushed Jaime's out of the way, and wrapped her arms around him in gratitude.

* * *

The spring breeze gently blew across Jaime's face as he stopped to sit on a bench along his routine walk home from campus.

Birds glided across the lake, and families gathered by the water and played with their little children. Jaime reclined comfortably in his seat and observed the world around him.

He had only one thought.

Time for another adventure.

ACKNOWLEDGMENTS

To create an exhaustive list of all those deserving credit for making this book possible would be difficult. Simply too many people have helped me bring these stories to life than there are pages to fit them. To those not named here who have helped in any way to the publication of this book, thank you.

Thank you to those who accompanied me on my travels—Winston, Kennidy, Mackenzie, Carol, and many others—I would not have learned these crucial life lessons if you all had not been there with me.

The love and support from my family has easily been the greatest motivator in finishing this book. Thank you to my wonderful parents and loyal siblings for always being my number one fans and believing in me in all of my pursuits, no matter how crazy they are. I especially want to thank my older brother and life mentor, Garret, for always answering the phone at any hour of the day to let me think out loud and for always giving me the advice I needed to hear.

A special thanks to the McGhie and Farley families, whose special generosity and confidence in me made this all possible.

I'd also like to gratefully acknowledge:

Jessica McGhie, Stetson Barschi, Lindsey Rendon, Melinda Maughan, Rachel Cowen, Maret Sotkiewicz, Sherri Jemley, Sarah Stewart, Saffron Snethen, David Walch, Sarah Aguilar de Escobedo, Annie Trumbull, Mckenna Crawford, Dallan Escobar, Emmali Day, William Okazaki, Elli Kennedy, Kylin Parker, Leeann Robey, Iraima Otteson, Ralf Wagner, Amy Antonelli, Bill Freedman, Lori Holden Scott, Aidan Reiri, Itza Miller, Jeff Derricott, Elle Campbell, Kenny Ahlstrom, Parker Primo Scott, Annie Lowe, Alyssa Jemley, Mckenna Williamson, Stephanie Carter, Nathan Black, Brett Ogata, Kaleb Evans, Daniel Bean, Sam Witus, Camila & Kaleib Richey, Logan McAllister, Claire Costanza, Megan Jemley, Luke Alcorn, Kenzie Lopes, Alba Fonseca, Tanner Johnson, Hana Dodd, Desiree and McKay Mitchell, Ali Blake, Laurie Tracy, Cate Carabine, Mitchell Rice, Kalen Potter, Taylor Redd, Carsen Kendall, Umaize Savani, Shannon Sperry, JoAnn Christensen, Jackson You, Ashley Mulford, Dale Garlitz, Jonah Duffin, Casey Dorrough, Eric Koester, and Ian Kahng.

APPENDIX

AUTHOR'S NOTE
- Adkins, Amy. "Millennials: The Job-Hopping Generation." Gallup. December 16, 2019. https://www.gallup.com/workplace/231587/millennials-job-hopping-generation.aspx.

- Bethune, Sophie. "Gen Z More Likely to Report Mental Health Concerns." Monitor on Psychology. American Psychological Association, January 2019. https://www.apa.org/monitor/2019/01/gen-z.

- Blue Cross, Blue Shield. "The Economic Consequences of Millennial Health." Published November 6, 2019. https://www.bcbs.com/sites/default/files/file-attachments/health-of-america-report/HOA-Moodys-Millennial-10-30.pdf.

CHAPTER 2
- AZ Quotes. "Phil Knight Quotes." Accessed November 23, 2020. https://www.azquotes.com/author/19946-Phil_Knight.

- Climbing Kilimanjaro. "Is Climbing Kilimanjaro Dangerous?" Accessed November 23, 2020. https://climbingkilimanjaro.info/is-climbing-kilimanjaro-dangerous/.

CHAPTER 3
- *Encyclopedia Britannica.* s.v. "Kiribati." Accessed November 20, 2020, https://www.britannica.com/place/Kiribati.

- *Encyclopedia Britannica.* s.v. "Tarawa." Accessed November 20, 2020, https://www.britannica.com/place/Tarawa.

CHAPTER 5
- Goodreads. "Joe Paterno Quotes." Accessed November 23, 2020. https://www.goodreads.com/author/quotes/591907.Joe_Paterno.

- Wooden, John. "Motivational Quotes." The Wooden Effect. Accessed November 23, 2020. https://www.thewoodeneffect.com/motivational-quotes/.

Made in the USA
Columbia, SC
30 April 2021